Ja[illegible]

I hope this
book gives you
a understanding of
the people of Bangladesh,
Please keep the people of
Bangladesh in your prayers.

Vicki

P.S. Rick wrote the last
chapter.

For my part I hope you
enjoy the last chapter

Rick

Really, God—Bangladesh?

A NURSE'S SPIRITUAL JOURNEY

Vicki Augustiniak, RN

Inspiring Voices books may be ordered through booksellers or by contacting:

Inspiring Voices
1663 Liberty Drive
Bloomington, IN 47403
www.inspiringvoices.com
1-(866) 697-5313

ISBN: 978-1-4624-0510-7 (sc)
ISBN: 978-1-4624-0511-4 (e)

Library of Congress Control Number: 2013901109

Printed in the United States of America

Inspiring Voices rev. date: 2/6/2013

To my husband, Rick: Thank you for your love and support and for our journeys together

To my children, Gina and Mark: I love you

To my grandchildren, Alyssa, Brittany, Gibson, and Barbara Ann: You are the joy in my life and God's blessing to me.

CONTENTS

FOREWORD

Vicki Augustiniak has been my companion on many different paths in my life. She has never faltered in her support, her compassion, and her determination. When she told me she was traveling to Bangladesh, I was not surprised. I knew that it was her goal to use her skills to assist others. Through her efforts, I have seen her grow in strength and resolve.

This book, these words, are inspired by Vicki's faith and the loving support of her spouse. As she brings forth these events for you to share, think of this woman, born and raised in Detroit, who traveled to the other side of the globe to bring help and hope to the people she has met. I am glad to share my friend with you.

Sharon Sienkiewicz Lotoczky
August 2012

CHAPTER 1:

The Early Years: My Childhood and My Family

I never started out to write a book. I was writing a journal for my husband. Because of the many experiences I have had, I believe I was meant to write the story. The book's subtitle, *A Nurse's Spiritual Journey*, explains why I chose to start from the beginning of my life. I don't think you can understand my spiritual journey without knowing my history so I start with.

There are three identifiers that nurses are told to use when giving medications to patients in the hospital. The first is the person's name. The second is the patient's ID number. The third is the patient's date of birth. So I start this book with those facts: My name is Victoria Kuczewski, and I was born on January 24, 1951. I am the oldest child of Bernard and Angeline Kuczewski.

I was born at St. Frances Hospital in Hamtramck, Michigan, near my home in Detroit. My history is that my father was the seventh of ten children. He had eight brothers and a sister. He was born in Mount Carmel, Pennsylvania, in 1927. He played football and wrestled. As a young man he joined the Marines and fought in World War II. After the war he moved to Michigan to work at the Chrysler factory. He met my mother at a dance, and they were married six months later.

My mother was the youngest of eight children. She grew up in Posen, Michigan. When she was two years old, her brother accidentally shot her in the chest with his BB gun. It was a miracle that she survived. My grandfather was so angry that my uncle hid for days.

My mother left school after the eighth grade. Her family was poor; they farmed on government land. She knew little of what was going on in the war. Her father was arrested during Prohibition for making moonshine and died in jail when she was nine years old. She moved from Posen to Detroit because there were no jobs in the smaller town; her sisters were already living there.

My parents had a troubled marriage. They were from different backgrounds. My mother was a simple farm girl who grew up without a father. My father was a city boy with big dreams. Many years later my father's cousin, Reggie, told me that my father wanted to leave my mother after I was born, but he was told that he had made his bed and he had to stay.

I remember them having many fights. My earliest memory was of my father lying on top of my mother, holding her down and telling us, "Don't do anything." I was about five years old at the time. My father drank too much. We never knew what state he would come home in. They would not fight every day, but the police often came to our house. The priest also came to our house. I remember standing in the alley and yelling at my father; I also remember pulling my father's hair to keep him from coming after my mother and hurting her.

All of this had a profound effect on me; being the oldest of nine, I looked for solutions. If only we were better. If only we had more money, a bigger house, but nothing I did made any difference. I hated how my mother was treated, and I often told her to leave; other times, I would tell her to stay. All of this made me feel very confused as a child.

Our house was built quickly after the war. My parents chose to buy a two-bedroom house with an upstairs income apartment. Aunt Stella loaned us money to buy the house, and she and her daughter, Barbara, lived there in a one-bedroom flat.

As our family grew, this two-bedroom house became too small. All five of us girls slept in one bedroom. Three of us slept in a double bed and two slept in a twin bed. We had one small closet. The boys had the other bedroom with triple bunks and a crib for my youngest brother. My parents slept on a sofa bed in the living room. My father worked midnights most of the time. We lived like this till I turned seventeen. At times we would have the gas turned off for non-payment in the summer, so my mother had to cook on a hot plate. We did not have a shower, so we could only take a bath. Every once in a while our toilet did not flush, and we would have to get a pan of water to use the toilet.

Our meals were homemade; my mother was a good cook. She worked so hard. She would wash our clothes with a ringer machine and rinse the clothes till the rinse water was clear. I caught my arm in the ringer helping my mother, twice that I can remember. Alcoholism affects many people. The summer before I became a senior, my parents had a big fight. My mother took five children to live with her brother Mike and their sister Anne, about five miles from our home. Because their house was so small, four of my siblings had to spend that summer at their friends' houses. To me, it felt like they were shipped off. Each of us went through much distress, as we were separated that summer.

My mother saw how difficult it was to stay with her sister, so we went back home and she and my father tried to make the marriage work, one more time. By this time, Aunt Stella and Barbara had moved into a rental down the street. When we moved back into the house, we now had the upstairs, and all of us were happier. I shared a room with only one sister at that time. We finally had two bathrooms. One day, my parents had a fight. My father kicked my mother in the mouth. My mother said, "He wouldn't kick a dog, but he kicked me!" Their marriage ended that day; they were divorced.

My father died a year after the divorce, alone in a hotel room. He was forty-seven years old when he died; my youngest brother was nine. Because of the divorce, I was the executor of the will and had to go to the lawyer to make sure that my brother and sister were taken care of. I also made funeral arrangements. I was twenty-three years old at the time.

My life as a child and teenager revolved around school and church. When I was seven years old, I became sick. I remember lying on the couch, watching "Milky Party Time," one minute and waking up in the hospital the next. I remember I was not afraid, even though my parents were not with me (at that time parents, could not stay with their children). I do remember a vision of a nun talking to my mother. The hospital had two wards with several children. I remember getting two shots a day, staying there for a week, and having no TV in my ward (we could not afford to pay for a TV). Two of the nurses were named Judy and Barbara, the same names as my sister and my cousin. The hospital was St. Frances, where I had been born. This illness occurred two weeks before making my First Holy Communion. I was allowed to make my communion even though I didn't practice and didn't practice for confession. I think because I was sick, making my communion was my first walk with Jesus. And even though I didn't know what I was doing, I gave my life to Jesus that day. This was important for me. This decision kept me from many of the pitfalls of being a child of the 60s and 70s.

I went to Holy Name of Jesus School from first grade through eighth grade. We studied religion and went to Mass every day. When I was young, Mass was in Latin, so we didn't understand what was being said. I loved sitting quietly in the church and reading about Jesus and about the saints. I loved knowing what things they did for Jesus. Some of them gave their lives to spread the good news about Jesus. I never wanted to be a martyr. I was too afraid for something like that. Those hours of quiet reflection, even as a child, were good for me. I had a lot of confusion at home and found some peace in church.

In 1965, Vatican Council met and life in the church changed. The altar was changed to face the people, and Mass was now in English. These changes were major, and the church became more open. We had guitar in Mass. The songs became more people friendly. The nuns dressed more like normal people. This was an exciting time to be a Catholic. Many people found these changes hard and questioned their faith, but I embraced them.

I went to St. Thomas High School. I was liked but really didn't fit there. Many of my good friends from grade school went there, like Jackie, who I first met when we were five years old, and Sharon, who I became friends with when we were twelve years old (both remain my best friends). In high school, again we studied religion and went to Mass weekly.

I also remember the Cuban missile crisis. We were all pretty scared. What would Russia do? Would they fire missiles at the United States? I was young but remember being fearful. In 1963, President John F. Kennedy was assassinated. I was in seventh grade and remember being in school when the announcement came. We were sent home from school early and were out of school for the next few days. All that was on the TV was about what had happened and about Kennedy's life. Our eyes were glued to the TV during the funeral. Life as we knew it had changed. We were vulnerable.

One day at class at Holy Name, an African American man came to speak to us about the plight of African Americans. At this time, African Americans were called Negros. This man helped change my thinking. Up to that time, I had no interaction with African Americans in my life. Like most of America, we lived in isolated communities. Polish people would come to America and stay with Polish people, Irish people would live with Irish people, Italians would stay with Italians. This happened mostly because of the language.

When I look back at this, I see how progressive it was to have this speaker come to our class. I will always remember what I learned that day: to look at things differently.

We didn't have a car, so usually we walked a mile to Holy Name; I took a bus to St. Thomas. If I chose to walk the mile and a half, I would have to go past a school with rough kids, and there were many fights. In 1967 Detroit had race riots. We lived in what was considered the inner city of Detroit. I do remember the riots. The governor called out the National Guard. Being a teenager and wanting to meet boys, we went up to where the guards were. What was a shock for me was that these young men were showing us young girls *Playboy* magazines. I had never seen a *Playboy* and didn't know what sex was. This was quite a shock for me.

I never had any boys interested in me; I was very shy, especially around boys. I now thank God for that because I was never tempted. Things were so different; going to Catholic school meant that our innocence was protected. In school, we could only read certain books, and we did not go see movies that were not allowed.

As far as the riots, I did remember my father not going to work for a few days; a couple of nights we heard gun shots. It was a scary few days. In 1968, the Detroit Tigers won the World Series, and Detroit was alive again. I worked after school at Detroit Bank and Trust. When the Tigers won the final game of the World Series, it was about 3:30. You could hear a roar after they won. The next thing we saw was paper flying out of the windows. Building after building, papers were flying. After I finished working, I walked down the street to find crowds of people having fun, yelling, blowing horns; there was even someone on the flag pole in Kennedy Square. I was very proud to live in Detroit that day.

Working downtown presented some challenges for me. I worked three days a week. Two of those days, Sharon worked with me, so she walked to the bus stop together. One day a week I walked alone. I worked till ten o'clock at night. We walked long city blocks in the cold breeze of the river to our bus stop, which was in front of a burlesque theatre. There were lots of posters of the girls outside. When I think of standing there at night, I still am amazed that nothing ever happened to us. Again I am grateful.

While in high school, I volunteered as a candy striper at St. Joseph Mercy Hospital. We would bring drinks to patients, take them to their rooms, spend time with them, and run errands. Our uniforms were white skirts with apron tops with red pinstripes, thus the name "candy stripers." I volunteered with Sharon and Jackie. I really enjoyed the time I spent doing this. I loved being in the hospital. This eventually motivated me to go into nursing.

My class was the last to graduate from St. Thomas. The school fought to stay open, but money drove that decision. My cousin Barbara and my sister Judy had to transfer to St. Cyril. I had wanted to be a nurse since I was in the hospital. This was the only thing I wanted to do. I briefly thought of being a stewardess but read a book that changed my mind; it seemed that stewardesses had a bad reputation. Later I would find out that nurses also had a bad reputation.

CHAPTER 2:

My Nursing Career

I tried to get into a nursing school in Kalamazoo, Michigan, but was not accepted. Uncle Mike drove me to the school for the testing and interview, and they told me right away that I would not be accepted. I remember crying all the way home because I was so disappointed. I now am grateful that I did not get into that school, because I would have been three hours away from my family, something I needed but emotionally was not ready for. God knew my needs.

I applied to Mercy School of Nursing of Detroit and was accepted. My father helped me apply to this school and went with me to the interview. This school was only four miles from home. I lived in the dorm but went home every weekend. I also worked as a cashier at K-Mart on the weekends. Nursing school was hard and the program was intense. By the grace of God, I graduated and became a nurse.

Here are some things I remember about nursing school: those of us who lived in the dorm had a curfew and couldn't have boys up in our rooms (not that I would have done that, but it was not allowed). My first year of school we went to class in Detroit. The school was down the street from the hospital. We started with a class of 120, and by the end of the year there were only 70 of us left. Some left because of grades, some left for personal reasons, and some left because they really didn't want to be nurses.

I was put in a special program for inner-city students and shared a room with an African American girl, Alesha. This was my first experience living with someone other than family. Alesha was a sweet girl; living with her taught me about other cultures, which helped me later in my life. Sometimes the tension of going to school and studying would bring out the playful side of us, and someone would be thrown into the bathtub with their clothes on, fighting all the way. The second year of school, we were split up into two different units, one at St. Joseph Hospital in Pontiac, Michigan, and the other at St. Joseph Mercy in Ann Arbor. I chose to stay at the Pontiac unit and still went home each weekend.

One of my best friends at that time was Susan. She would drive me home on the weekends. She later got married and worked in OB, and she was there for the birth of my son, Mark. During our psychiatry rotation, we all had to spend eight weeks in Ann Arbor. We lived in apartments. For most of us, this meant freedom. Nobody at the front desk, watching our every move. I turned twenty-one while I was in Ann Arbor. This was bittersweet for me, because that year, the laws were changed so that you could drink legally at eighteen. We celebrated while I was on that rotation. I do remember drinking Boone's Farm wine.

I also remember feeling like I didn't fit in with my friends; I felt they were smarter and had better lives. I really had a lot of insecurities, which came out at this time. While on this rotation, my case study patient was a fifty-year-old depressed alcoholic who committed suicide. My instructor was afraid to tell me. I think she was afraid I would feel like I could have done something different. I felt bad, but I remember thinking that if the physiatrist could not help him, what could I do? I was just a nursing student.

Three months before I graduated, I went on a blind date with the man who would become my husband. The husband of a friend of mine worked with Rick and arranged the date. Signals were crossed and the first week we didn't meet. Rick took me to the Playboy Club (this was not really Rick's personality). He came on strong, and I really was not sure about him; I even stood him up on one date. Just before graduation, I was having some problems in one of my classes, and Rick was there for me. He was so supportive and understanding, and that's when I fell in love with him.

We were married on November 2, 1973. Before the wedding, we attended Engaged Encounter, a premarital program. That decision helped us have a long and successful marriage. One of the things I remember about our wedding day is that it rained, a downpour, just after I got my hair done. The hard part of that day was that I got dressed at Rick's parents' house. When I got to Rick's house, he was there. They say the bride shouldn't see the groom before the wedding, so I waited in the car until he left.

For some reason, when we ordered the flowers, we forgot to order a white carpet. When the flowers arrived at Rick's parents' house, there was no white carpet, and I started to cry. First of all, I was uncomfortable having to dress for my wedding at my future in-laws' house. I felt once again I didn't fit in, and I didn't have a normal family. Second, I always wanted to walk down the aisle on a white carpet.

Thank God, my sister Chris helped me call around and find a white carpet. After we found one, I called Rick and he said he would pick it up, but due to poor planning I was never able to walk down a white carpet. But in the end it wouldn't make any difference.

Uncle Mike gave me away, as my father did not attend the wedding. I had a hard decision to make, as my parents were in the process of divorcing (their divorce was final the month after my wedding). I wrote a letter to my father and asked him to give me away. He did not reply right away, and so I had asked my uncle. I had written the letter because even though he was still living in the house, the tension was so severe that we didn't speak. I would later come to know that silence in a home where people don't talk can be as damaging as fights.

Uncle Mike was very good to me. He was never married and had no kids of his own; sometimes he gave me more time than my father. My father finally replied by mail, telling me that he could not take the day off of work because he was close to losing his job. He also said that he would have a Mass said for us.

A month after the wedding, a Mass was said for us; my father had kept his word. That meant (and still means) a lot to me. I would only see him one more time before his death. He died alone in a hotel room, without his family. I now know that this was not something he wanted for his life.

After the wedding, we drove to the reception; Rick was so sweet. He was happy and kept kissing me. I had found someone who loved me. At the reception, Rick had the DJ play a song for him to sing to me: "Let me call you sweetheart, I'm in love with you." I know it was corny, but I loved it and can't hear that song without remembering him singing that as we danced.

Both Rick and I credit the Engaged Encounter with the success of our marriage. It wasn't just going to the Encounter, it was the decision to work on the program. At the Encounter, we found our spiritual parents, David and Ruth. I was so nervous at first around them. David and Ruth had gone through Marriage Encounter and enjoyed what they learned, but they said their marriage would have been easier if they had gone to Engaged Encounter. At Marriage Encounter, couples spent a weekend away to look at themselves first and their partners next. Topics included communication, signs of spiritual divorce, sex, independence, reconciliation with past, and goals. This gave couples time to look at the marriage and not just the wedding day. At the Encounter, we learned that God had given us two important times: the Sabbath and marriage. The Encounter promoted godly marriages between a man and women. Rick and I tried to take at least one Encounter a year, usually in November for our anniversary. The material for the Encounter was always changing, and David and Ruth added new insights from their experiences and also from the couples who worked on the Encounter. One of the exercises involved couples writing out their one year, five year and ultimate goals for housing, spiritual life, family, education, and so on. One year in November, Rick and I wrote our housing goal: owning a four-bedroom ranch house on a lake. Today, we live in a four-bedroom ranch house with a pool (I tell people that God knew I really don't like the muck of a lake and that's the reason we have a pool; he knew our needs).

Because of my background, at first I did not feel good enough around David and Ruth. I came from this chaotic house, and they seemed to have everything together. Rick and I both wanted a good marriage. We knew that God wanted that same thing for us. We gave ourselves to a covenant marriage. It wasn't perfect; we made (and still make) mistakes, but God was included in our marriage. Once when we were having a hard time, David said, "At least you two love each other." We learned about forgiveness, which is very important in a marriage. David and Ruth mentored us. They honestly told what they saw. David was so gifted spiritually. He read Scripture and knew God's word. Together they wrote some great insights into Christian marriage. We went though many prayer meetings and shared many meals with them. David was always searching for God's truths. They had seven children, so their lives were busy. Watching them and seeing that their children were not perfect would help me later in life. I am so grateful that they took the time to help us. They always had time for us.

The love we received from them was just what I needed. I remember being at their house one day; Ruth was taking care of my children and I was resting with the Bible on my chest. Some of my treasured memories include being at their house on a lake. Their house was a peaceful place for me. We still have a special place in our hearts for the Engaged Encounter couples and their families. Ruth died shortly after my mother passed away. David remained single for about six years and then married a wonderful woman named Karen. Even after Ruth's death, David remained in our life.

My first job was at St. Joseph Mercy in Detroit, where I had trained. My boss was a tough old Army nurse. I was in charge of the nursing aides, including an older Africa-American nursing aide. My boss ran a tight ship, and everyone respected her. I had so much to learn. Giving meds for a team of twelve to thirteen patients was hard. I saw my first death on that floor, a man who had just come to our floor. He had to go to the bathroom for a bowel movement; he had a cardiac arrest and was coded and died.

I was challenged as a young nurse when I did a midnight rotation. When I reported for duty, there was an African American woman who had a major stroke and needed to be put on a ventilator. There was no room in ICU, so she stayed with us for the night. I was four weeks out of nursing school. There were two nurses for the unit, thirty patients, and I was working with a licensed practical nurse (LPN). This LPN was more experienced than me, but since I was the RN, I was in charge. We split the floor that night along with this patient; I would check on her on the hour, and the LPN would check on her on the half hour. That was how we survived the night; the stroke patient made it through the night okay. Since then, I have often told new nurses, "If the patient is alive at the end of your shift, it's been a good day." That evening I really meant it. I think if she had died, I would have quit nursing.

One funny thing that happened (though you might not agree that it's funny) was that a nurse aide put a glass thermometer into a patient's mouth; he was a confused older man, and he bit down on the thermometer and swallowed it. The thermometer contained mercury, so we worried that he might get brain damage, but since he was older, we were more worried about the glass going through his bowels and cutting him. We monitored his bowel movements (this meant going through his bowel movements), and eventually he passed the thermometer. Doesn't the job of checking his bowel movements sound like fun? This is the life of nurses and nursing aides. What really made me upset was that even after we posted a large sign above his bed warning about this issue, another aide tried to put a glass thermometer in his mouth again; he tried to bite this one too but did not swallow it this time.

One of my most embarrassing moments came as I was trying to be effective and to imitate my coworkers. In those days, medications were passed out on a metal tray. We also used little cards to tell which drugs were to go to which patients. The cards had patients' names, room number, and medication, with dose. We would pass out medications at nine o'clock and one o'clock. My coworkers (who had much more experience than me) would set up their tray with meds for both doses, the nine o'clock dose on top in meds cups, the one o'clock underneath. Because I was new, I didn't do this. I noticed how they worked and tried out a different method (what I thought was a better way). Doing this took me longer than normal. I was trying to make sure I had everything right. I didn't start passing my meds till 9:30, already a half hour later. My tray had a bottle of Maalox for ulcer patients. I was able to pass meds in the first room to two of my patients. The Maalox did not balance very well and the tray fell, along with all the medications in it. I was so embarrassed and frightened. I wanted to do everything right. I wanted to be this great nurse. I had to start over with the medications and was late getting my medications out. I can tell you that these things can still make me feel bad, but I have learned to move on.

Most nurses recall the things that they do not do perfectly. We can be really hard on ourselves, and I believe most doctors could say the same thing. We spend a lot of time going over how we could do better, both privately and in reviews. I spent a year and a half on this medical-surgical floor learning how to be a nurse.

Some of the nurses I worked with were from the Philippines. I remember going to lunch with a whole table of Filipino nurses with then speaking their language and feeling left out. This was my first encounter with Asian people, but as you will see, it was not my last. God was preparing me for what I would experience later in life.

I transferred to the pediatrics unit in the same hospital. I always wanted to work with children. This was a small unit; we didn't have many patients. There was a head nurse, two nurse aides, and myself. I was hired there with the understanding that I would float if we didn't have patients.

During this time, I met a patient who helped me learn what nursing really meant. Wendy was an African American girl and about eleven years old. She had a brain injury and her legs were bent across her abdomen. She could not walk and used a wheelchair; she often had infections and sores. Her doctors finally decided to remove her legs. After her surgery, I was blessed to take care of her. Wendy had a great personality and was a joy to take care of. One day, I took her to visit the Detroit Zoo in her wheelchair; we had some fun that day. This was what I became a nurse for.

I became pregnant with my daughter while I was working on this unit and took three months off. When I returned, I no longer worked on the unit and floated to all the units in the hospital. My work just got harder and less rewarding. The worst floor was the GYN floor, where again I was the RN working with LPN's (there was no head nurse). The

LPN's I worked with resented me. This unit also was a culture shock to me. The patients were mostly African Americans from the inner city with a lot of pain issues.

I continued in this floating position for a few months and then accepted a position at Children's Hospital of Michigan (CHM). I told the recruiter that I didn't want to work with babies, but I was placed in the neonatal intensive care unit (NICU). Again, I look back at what I thought was a mistake and see God's hand. I was still too quiet to make a fuss and did what I was told. I ended up learning so much. I took care of babies, small babies. I worked afternoons at first, so we needed someone to watch Gina, our daughter, for a short time, and then I went to midnights.

What I liked about working at CHM was that everyone had ideas worth listening to. The doctors respected the nurses, asked our opinions, and included us in rounds. The doctors knew that we spent all day with the patients. I learned how to gavage babies, feed cardiac infants, and give meds; nurses didn't start IVs, but we would hold the babies for the residents to start IVs.

I learned so much and took care of almost every abnormality a baby can be born with. I took care of infants with spinal bifida, choanal atresia, billiary atresia, Pierre robin, prune belly, osteogenesis imperfect, epidermolysis bullosa, all forms of Trisomy, omphalocele, all kinds of cardiac anomalies, and metabolic disorders. We treated conjoined (Siamese) twins and many premature babies.

We did not have pulse oximentry machines in those days, so infants were weaned off oxygen by blood gases. As a result, many premature infants developed bronchopulmonary dysplasia (BPD). I took care of two babies with BPD. One baby, Jonathan, was a triplet; his sister Mary died, his sister Catherine did well and he was sent home on oxygen. I later heard that Jonathan did well.

My other primary baby was Mandy, who stayed with us till he was six months old. Mandy had severe BPD and was always on oxygen. We tried to wean him off oxygen by blood gasses; he would be at 23 percent for a few days and then would go into respiratory distress and have to go back on oxygen. This went on day after day. Mandy eventually died, and I went to the funeral. I took his death hard; nurses always feel they could have done something better.

I also took care of babies who had necrotizing enterocolitis (NEC). We were just starting to learn about NEC. Some of our babies would end up with colostomies and short gut syndrome. I remember one premature girl, approximately thirty-three weeks old; she was what we called a growing preemie. She was in an isolette but stable, being gavage fed. At midnight we started getting some of the formula feedings back, and her belly blew up. At 6:30, she arrested and died; her intestine had probably ruptured.

This made such an impact on me because preemies were fed formula, which can increase the incidence of perforation of the intestines. I became a breast-feeding consultant and always encouraged preemie moms to breast-feed.

One of the things I loved about working at CHM was that I went on ambulance rounds to pick up infants at different hospitals. Whenever I got to go, the excitement junky came out in me. Usually at work, I did not want excitement. I liked the calm. Going to different hospitals gave me a chance to see other places and made me feel important.

One time I went to a hospital in Canada to pick up a baby. Going across the border was exciting. This was long before 9/11, so we didn't even have to show our passports. Another time, we picked up a child who had epiglottitis (this is a potentially lethal swelling of the epiglottis, which can completely obstruct the airway). That was one of the scarcest runs I went on, as we took a tracheotomy set in case we had to perform emergency surgery in the ambulance. The doctor, respiratory therapist, and I watched the child in his mother's arms the whole way.

I worked at CHM for six years. Our son Mark was born while I worked there. I loved the work even though it was hard. We would take care of four to six babies at a time. I would have stayed there but I was young and did not like the management. They asked me to become permanent but never got back to me, so I got upset, took it personally, and quit. I always think fondly of my time at CHM and was glad I worked there. I learned so much.

Working at CHM was helpful to my family when my sister Fran

gave birth to my nephew Joey. He was transferred to CHM right after birth for pulmonary, heart, and billiary astesia. When he was six month old, he had open heart surgery, but he died. The night before his death, Fran and I stayed at Ronald McDonald House. Watching him die was difficult for me; as a nurse, I knew that he had a very poor chance of survival. It was also hard to see all the tubes and IVs. The hardest part of that day was when we got the call, telling us to come back to the hospital; Fran knew that Joey had died; she walked to his room with her other children at her side, knowing she was facing the loss of a child.

I soon became dissatisfied with management at CHM and looked in the newspaper, where I saw an ad for a midnight pediatric nurse at Beaumont Hospital in Troy. This was a small suburban hospital. They had been without a midnight nurse for seven months, and I had worked with the head nurse at CHM. I took this challenging job, where I was the only nurse on the midnight shift for a seventeen-bed unit.

The children's ages went from newborn to eighteen. Patients usually came here for asthma, croup, hernia repair, or appendectomies. I worked for what I considered the best head nurse. She was quite detailed but was fair. She did not have favorites. I found working for her I wanted to be my best. She worked hard, and if we needed her, she would roll up her sleeves and pitch in.

One night after I had been at the hospital about three months, the midnight supervisor called to ask how many patients we could take, because a school camp was reported to have carbon monoxide poisoning. I thought that he was playing a joke on me because I was the new kid. I asked him three times if this was a joke. He assured me that it was not a joke. I did not know about carbon monoxide poisoning and had to look it up. Since I was the only nurse that night, I was really frightened. When we did not get any patients from the camp, I was relieved.

Because I was the only nurse, I could only take my lunch break when the supervisor relieved me; this meant that if she was busy or if I got a new patient, I did not get a break. Working at this new hospital was quite a culture shock. I was used to inner-city people and had never met such snobby people. My coworkers often discussed their new houses, vacations, designer clothes, and many more material things. I was shocked one day when someone asked my co-worker if that was a "Coach purse?" I didn't know what a coach purse was let alone own one. I got very upset one day when someone said that if she won the lottery, she would buy a new house and a new car but never mentioned giving any money to help the poor.

I worked with a great nurse aide (she became a nurse later). If I had not worked with such skilled nurse aides, I would not have been able to stay there. We also had a great secretary, Carol, who many a night would watch the children at the desk. Because of the night crew, I enjoyed my work but always felt insecure around the day shift.

We took care of a young man named Dan, who was eighteen years old when he fell at a construction site and became paralyzed from the neck down. We took care of him for about a month. My nursing assistant and I would turn him two or three times a night. He also had to be catheterized twice a night. Night was hard for him; he had a lot of fears at night. My nurse assistance and I spent many nights talking to him and listening to his fears. I remember how hard it was for him because he couldn't blow his nose and we had to clean his nose.

One of the other patients had lost his toes after a firecracker accident. The firecracker did not go off, and because there were small children around, he decided to step on it to keep them from getting hurt. Several toes were blown off. He had to walk on crutches. He had a great spirit but regretted stepping on the firecracker.

We also had a young girl who was challenging because she refused to eat; she had a fractured femur and was in traction. We tried everything to get her to eat.

I also remember a young man who was pinned in the back of a car to a wall and had an open wound that went down to his bone. His dressing changes were difficult.

CHAPTER 3:

Life Is Not Perfect and Neither Are Families

During this time, I found myself dealing with some personal issues and sought help in a twelve-step program. What a blessing; again, God knew my needs. By this time in my life, I was like Much-Afraid, the character in the book *Hinds' Feet on High Places* by Hannah Hurdard. I learned so much in the program (and I am still learning). I learned "Let Go and Let God," "Live and Let Live," "Just for Today," and "Think." I learned that just because I make a mistake, it does not mean I am a mistake. I found a place where I could just be me. I would be loved just because, not because of what I could do.

Because of what I had lived with growing up, I needed a place to talk and be listened to. I was tired of taking care of everyone but myself. My family had placed demands on me. I was the oldest, the most responsible. Many of those who go into nursing fit this description. We become good at helping others; after all, we are in a helping profession.

I had God in a box. I thought if you loved God, life was perfect, and when it wasn't, I was angry. But I kept my anger inside. I let other people behavior affect my joy and peace. I had read somewhere that your parents and family should give you "roots and wings." When I looked at my past, I saw my roots entwined with everyone; they were very fragile and thin. If you pulled them out, everyone came with them. I looked at my wings as heavy and large, like angel wings; if you opened them up, there were people hidden under them, hiding.

At this time I my life, Rick and I had lived with my mother twice, trying to make her life and ours easier. My brothers and sisters had been affected by alcoholism, and they were making poor choices, just like me. This was one of the lowest points of my life. I had a lot of personal work to do on myself. I learned so much about myself. I learned to used the Serenity Prayer and also used something called the Golden Key, which teaches that instead of worrying about things you cannot control, you should think about God. I was still going to church, but my angry and self-pity were eating me up.

Fortunately, we moved away from my mother before she died. It would have been harder to go through her dying while we lived there. I am grateful that I had a great mother; her death taught me so much. She had called me the day before she died to discuss something we found hard to talk about, and initially I was angry. Eventually, though, I talked to her, and that was the last time I talked to my mother.

The next day, Gina called me at work to say that my mother was sick and was being transported to the hospital. I left work and went to the hospital; when I saw her pass by on the stretcher, I could tell by her coloring that she was not doing well. My sister and brother met me at the hospital. We went into a conference room, and the doctor told us that my mother had a ruptured cerebral aneurysm and a sub-dural hematoma. I started to cry and had to explain what that meant to my sister and brother. The doctors wanted to put her on a ventilator, but I knew that my mother did not want that.

I went to my brother and sister and we discussed what to do; I was not an only child, and they would have to help with this decision. They could not process what had happened, so my mother went on a ventilator. That turned to be the right decision, as my sister Judy, who lived in Arizona, was able to fly to Michigan and see our mother alive. She would later say that seeing her one more time was comforting to her. Eventually, my mother was removed from the ventilator. I have never known such grief. I sobbed and sobbed. I would be somewhat okay until I was alone, and then I would break down again. I remember seeing my oldest friend Jackie at the funeral I saw; my mother loved Jackie, and I broke down and sobbed in her arms.

The week after my mother's death I went to a meeting and asked to have a Step 3 (Make a decision to turn our will and our lives over to the care of God as we understood him). One of my friends, Laura, had come late, and I told her to sit by me. Her mother had also died suddenly. Even today, both of us discuss how we are feeling at the time of year of our mother's death.

After the funeral, I went through my mother's purse and found a handwritten will; to my surprise, I was not mentioned in the will. I handed the will to my sister and went off by myself to process this.

I did not fall apart till I got home. I felt abandoned by my mother. I didn't matter. I was the only child not included. Me, the daughter who worked hard to please my mother; many times in my life, I had put her needs before myself, my husband, and my children. When we moved, she had given us some money, but she never told me that I was excluded from her will. I would have felt so much better if she had told me. I felt ashamed. What kind of daughter was I to be left out of her will?

I called Ruth to help me sort this out. She asked me how my mother and I had been getting along. I told her we were getting along well; it had been two years since we moved. She told me that my mother was a Christian and that she probably had gotten angry one day and wrote the will; she added that it was done, and I had to look at how she treated me. She also told me that I had choices: I could fight this or accept the will. She also told me that my family had choices that were out of my hands.

My family decided to let the will stand but allowed me to take some personal items belonging to my mother that I wanted. I took my mother's bread bowl, a picture I embroidered for her, a bear I gave her at Christmas, her cake decorating pans, and many more things that I wanted to pass on to my children. I learned much about acceptance in this process. I knew that things happened as they were supposed to; I do not carry guilt about living with my mother now. I took comfort in my meetings more than ever at this time.

The hospital opened an obstetrics unit, and it went to full occupancy right away. The unit was only staffed for 60 percent occupancy, and pediatrics nurses were often pulled over to that unit. I was so excited but also scared. I had not seen a baby being born since nursing school, some seventeen years before. One day I saw three babies being born; what a high I was on that day!

I learned to "catch" babies (take care of them after birth) and help mothers recover after giving birth. I really enjoyed working on this unit. At this time, a position opened up on days. I wanted to go to days, as I had worked about eighteen years on the night shift.

I loved working nights but never saw myself doing this the rest of my life. The daytime position went to someone with less seniority than me. I felt this was wrong and went to grievance about this. That was quite a process. I accepted a part-time position and a contingent position at NICU at Royal Oak (a bigger hospital with a high level of NICU). About a month later, there was an opening in the midnight special care nursery (SCN), and I accepted this position and moved to SCN. It was hard to stay on midnights but I knew that there would be more chance to move to days eventually. Again God knew my needs; because of this move, I met Dr. Lee, and my story would begin.

At this time, I endured what became the hardest part of my life. One day, as I was about to walk out the door for work, Mark, our sixteen-year-old son, told Rick and me that Jenny, his fifteen-year-old girlfriend, was pregnant. I really don't know how I made it to work that day or how I worked that night. If it had not been for a coworker helping me that night, I would have fallen apart. Unless you have heard these words spoken to you, you really can't imagine the pain. Rick and I went through many feelings: what would we do, what would happen to Mark, what would happen to our grandchild; we felt guilt for not protecting our child, we felt guilt for not telling him enough times not to have sex till he got married, we felt shame for him not being perfect.

For me, this was like the shame I had lived with most of my life. Three of my sisters had had babies without being married. Judy was pregnant at her high school graduation. Mary was seventeen when she became pregnant; she and her daughter lived with us for a year and a half. Fran joined the Army, and the night before she left for boot camp, she told me she thought she was pregnant. She left the next day and was sent home about a month later, pregnant.

I found myself in a very low place and decided to tell my three sisters all in one day; I was a wreck. I cried. I found myself almost unable to get out of bed. I did not understand how this could happen to my family. I felt so alone and such shame. Thank God I had some great friends who let me have my feelings; they did not tell me I was wrong for these feelings. They gave me love and support. David and Ruth also helped me get through it. I tried to contact Jenny's mom to help her, but she did not want to meet with us.

I found comfort in saying the rosary. Some people feel that we shouldn't use repetitive prayers, but this helped me. When I got over the shock, I tried to look for solutions to help the kids and my future grandchild. We sat down with Mark and Jenny and discussed their options. We saw three choices: adoption, us raising the child, or the kids raising the child. The first choice was the only one I liked.

Catholic Social Services offered free counseling to pregnant teenagers, so every week I picked up Jenny (she lived some twenty miles away) and drove her and Mark to counseling. She had told us that her mother had said that if she kept the child, she could not live with her, but her father had offered to take her in (her parents had divorced when Jenny was five).

We suggested that she move in with him before the baby was born to see if it would work, so that the day after the baby was born she would not be left on the street if he changed his mind. She moved in with her father before the baby was born. We also took Jenny and Mark to meet with a couple who were looking to adopt and with someone who had given their baby up for adoption. Mark, Rick, and I remained in counseling, and I went to see a counselor on my own.

It was a blessing that our daughter was away at college so she did not go through what was going on at our house. I was also angry at my son. Three people offered to adopt the baby. I begged Mark to give this child up for adoption. I tried everything I could do for this to happen. Rick took Mark to see David, who also told Mark that adoption was the best choice.

A friend had given me a Life Recovery Bible at this time. I had always found it hard to read the Bible and had never understood the Old Testament. I was in so much pain that I started to read the Bible. I found great hope in what I read. I discovered that the people in the Old Testament were not perfect; they made lots of poor choices. I began to have hope for my son, as I discovered that the line Christ was born from had children born outside of wedlock.

Despite everything we said, the kids decided to keep the child. Mark had a dream that he and Jenny would marry and be together forever. Accepting all of this was hard. I leaned on the Serenity Prayer most of the time. Before the baby was born, I had decided not to be present at the birth. I was afraid that if I saw the child, I would have to raise him, and because marriage is hard, I didn't know if that would be the best for the child. I was also still very angry at both of the kids. I knew that a sixteen-year-old girl did not need someone who was angry at her at the birth of her child.

Jenny's mom finally agree to be with her during the birth. Mark and I talked about it beforehand, and I agreed to take him to Jenny's so they could go to the hospital together. I struggled when I had to leave my seventeen-year-old to go through this life-changing process alone. I wanted to take him in my arms and make it all better. I told him I would go with him if he wanted, but he said that he would be all right. I cried most of the way home and am crying as I write this. I was able to hug him and tell him I loved him.

Of course, because I was not ready, the baby came three weeks early. Mark was involved in high school wrestling at this time and had to miss a meet when Alyssa was born in January. The day that Alyssa was born, I was very upset and went to a meeting, where I was sobbing in the arms of my friend. The funny thing about this was my friend had been a mother at seventeen years old.

That March, Mark became state wrestling champ in his weight class. What a year of highs and lows. We were proud of him for winning the state title. At this point, we still had not seen the baby. I still hoped that the reality of taking care of a child might prove to be too much for Jenny and she would decide to give Alyssa up, plus I knew we could not raise her as our child. At this point in my life, I knew I could not rescue my son for the consequences of his behavior. This was tough love but it was needed for Mark to mature. Mark was going to school, working, and seeing Alyssa when he could. Thank God, Mark had a supportive wrestling coach. I will always be grateful to him.

The day after Mark won the championship, there was an article about him in the local paper. This article mentioned Alyssa. I had not told the people I worked with because I was ashamed, but there it was in print, and there was nothing I could do about it. I used the Serenity Prayer to help me accept that my friends would know about my son not being perfect.

Right around this time, I went to a 12 step program convention that Jenny and Alyssa were also attending. We had not yet seen Alyssa, so I was living in fear of this. At this convention, there was a topic table on fear, and I chose to sit there. I went through all my fears and anger about my situation. I felt a lot of self-pity about what had happened to my son. The person sitting next to me began to talk, she shared that her son had gotten two women pregnant and they were due two months apart. I was in shock and told myself that it could have been worse. Dealing with what she was going through would have been harder. God once again showed me something that I needed to hear. I saw this woman several times after this, and we shared our stories. I never forgot this lesson.

Mark graduated in June. He and Jenny had broken up; this occurred right after we saw Alyssa for the first time. Mark had taken Alyssa for the weekend, and we helped him take care of her. I was numb and kept my feelings in check. I didn't instantly connect with her. I did what I needed to do, but the joy a grandparent feels was not there. She was something I had not planned in my life or my child's life. Rick handled this much better.

As time went on, Mark would drive thirty miles every other weekend to pick Alyssa up at Jenny's father's house. According to Mark, the couple broke up because Jenny "changed." Imagine that! I bet you didn't see that coming. Mark did take Jenny to prom; her mother had suggested that, adding that it might be the only time she could go to prom.

About a year later, Jenny's father moved to Tennessee. I am not sure what plans Jenny had at this time, but the next thing we heard was that she was pregnant again and would marry the father of this baby. I remember the day Mark found out; he went out to his punching bag and used it to get his anger out. He was angry at himself because he always thought Jenny would marry him. Even though Jenny married someone else, Mark still picks Alyssa up every other weekend and continues to be in her life. My mother-in-law has said to me many times, "Aren't you glad that Alyssa is in your life?" I always answer her the same way: "It's isn't about me. Alyssa needed to be taken care of."

I have always thought it would have been better if Jenny and Mark had been older so they could have been married. Alyssa would have been raised by both her mother and her father. Alyssa is now a joy in my life, she loves me and I know it. I can now say I love her. We love to shop together. She lives thirty miles away but we do see her and she is a part of our lives. Now that she is a teenager, I am a little afraid about her future. One of the hard parts in this is I have no relationship with Jenny. We see each other infrequently, but she is not my daughter-in-law. She is just Alyssa's mom. This is not my choice. I have tried to reach out to Jenny, but she has put up walls.

The thing I am grateful for is that Jenny has never kept us from seeing Alyssa. We have taken her on vacation several times. The one regret I have is that I didn't keep a diary at the time, which could have helped other parents whose sons became fathers at a young age. As I write this, I want you to know that even though this happened, I am proud of my son. He is a good father and loves his daughter. He talks to her and is someone she can go to. I believe he has done what God wanted him to do.

I was a child of the 60s, and one of the things President Kennedy started was physical fitness programs. I played basketball and baseball, and I like being active. I never learned to swim; in fact, I was scared of the water. The closest pool to our house as a kid was a mile and a half away and cost money, so we didn't go very often. One of my friends tried holding me up in the water, I guess trying to teach me, but she let go of me and I thought I was going to drown. My fear of water was great, but I also loved being near the water.

When Rick and I first got married, I took swimming lessons. It took me forever to learn to float on my back. I learned to conquer my fear and felt great about that. I committed to swimming once a week. I discovered water aerobics and loved exercising in the water. I could get a great workout without sweating. I also tried to swim a few laps in the pool. It took me some time to work up to ten lengths of the pool. I kept swimming and increased time at the pool as the kids got older. One day I told my friend that I felt bad because I was swimming but wasn't praying enough. She said, "Why don't you pray in the water?" My first thought was, I can't do that, I can barely swim. I liked and trusted this person. But I dispelled what she said. My old negative self came through. I thought, *You didn't even try what she said to you.* So I tried and tried.

By that time, I was swimming about forty-four lengths of the pool (my age). My goal at that time was to add a length for every year I lived. When I decided to pray in the water, I thought I couldn't do long prayers. Too hard! So I said a simple prayer: "God bless ___." I filled in the blank with my husband, daughter, son, Alyssa and Jenny, Rick's parents. About three months later, I was swimming a mile (seventy-two lengths of that pool). I was so excited; this was something I never thought I could do. It is amazing what prayer can do. Now what was I to do? Swim two miles? I did that within the year. I added two lengths a month, still praying. What happened next was something I did not expect.

If I was angry, had resentment toward someone, or was worried about something, it came out in the water. I was given a new freedom I didn't have before. I also stopped trying to figure out someone else's life. I could pray for someone and let go of the results. I had people asking me to pray for them. I was also told by a fellow swimmer that I look like I was meditating. I was doing Step 11 (Sought through prayer and meditation to improve our conscious contact with God as we understood Him, praying only for the knowledge of His will for us and the power to carry that out). After I swam two miles, what was next?

I made a goal to swim three miles (216 lengths of that pool) for my fiftieth birthday. I had decided that I couldn't do this just once but would swim this distance three times a week for one month, so that I could say that I could swim three miles. I did reach that goal for my fiftieth birthday.

My only regret was that I did not lose any weight, not one pound. I then talked to personal trainers who told me to start lifting weights, which I started and continue today. I still swim and do water aerobics and do treadmill and bike. I did not make three miles for my sixtieth birthday but did about 160 lengths. After three miles, I had no thought of going to four miles. Sometimes I feel like I am bragging when I say how much I swim, but I could not do this without God's help, and I am trying to encourage all people that we can sometimes push ourselves beyond what we think we can do.

One of the blessings I had doing water aerobics was meeting Joanne, my water aerobics instructor. Joanne is a Christian, and we often talk about spiritual matters. The first time she invited me to a Bible study, I told her I was too busy (which was the truth). I am so grateful that she did not give up on me. Studying the Bible has opened up a whole new world to me. Joanne taught me not to give up on people.

Another blessing in my life was a family reunion in 2000. This reunion was on my father's side of the family. The "Y2K(uczewski)" reunion was held in Mount Carmel, in the family home where my father grew up. Two of my cousins arranged it, and we had a good time. The house was on N. Locust Street. My grandmother raised nine boys and one girl without a bathroom in the house, just an outhouse. I had stayed at this house twice in my life. We visited my grandmother when I was eight years old for Christmas one year, and when my grandmother died, my father took me there, so visiting this house brought back memories. In the room where my grandmother slept was a picture frame with prayer cards of people who had died. These cards were old; they also told me something about my grandmother.

I sat and talked to my cousin about the alcoholism that had been in her family with her father. We both tried to heal in this home and with each other. We also toured the coal mines, and I could see why my father chose to leave Pennsylvania and move to Michigan. He did not want to spent his life working in the coal mines. My uncle shared something I did not know as we toured the cemetery where my grandmother was buried. He said that even though my grandmother had no formal training, she often went to houses where TB was present and nurse the people. Three of her grandchildren became nurses.

While at the reunion, we went to Mass as a family, and it was there that I discovered the depth of my grandmother's faith. Seven of her sons served overseas during World War II, and she went to Mass every day. All of her sons, including my father, returned home safely. I also discovered at this Mass that my grandmother prayed not only for her children but for her grandchildren, and I am blessed because of these prayers.

After the reunion, something happened in the world that changed life in the United States: September 11, 2001. Like all of us, I remember what I was doing that day. I was working in OB and had gone to our break room for my morning break. The TV was on, showing the airplane going into the first tower. What a shock! We had patients to take care of so, we would go in and out, trying to see what was happening. Some of the patients were watching their TVs, so we could get an update. But because of what we do, the patients come first, so we continued to do our jobs. We were nervous, especially when we were told that hospitals had to be on high alert.

When a tragedy like this happens, I know that as a nurse, I might be called on to help people in need. I have heard young nurses say if a tornado happened, they would leave the hospital to go be with their families, and I can't understand this. I would hope that there would be hospital staff to take care of my family if they were injured. I could do nothing to help them if I left the hospital.

We all saw the second plane hit the other tower, we all saw the plane hit the Pentagon, we knew that a fourth plane was headed for the White House, we all saw the towers come down, and we all saw the terror in people's eyes.

One of the nurses was shaken, because she had visited New York the week before and had gone to the World Trade Center; she could have been in the buildings when the airplanes hit. We saw how people came together. The churches were filled, people were praying. The shock was that the people who did this had lived in this country next to us. How can you justify this? When things like this happen, I remember the slogan "One day at a time," because we are not guaranteed another day.

Mark came to us one day and asked if his friend Reina could move in with us. He expected that we would say no, but he had promised his friend he would ask, and he kept his word. Reina was a friend from high school. Mark took her to the prom because her fiancé was twenty-eight years old and did not want to go. Reina and her parents were supportive of Mark with Alyssa. Her parents even babysat for Alyssa. We were at a place where I was busy and couldn't keep the house clean, so I saw the chance to have someone help us. Reina was in a bad relationship, and because she was an only child, she felt that if she went home there would be discord with her parents. We agreed that she could move in and help us keep the house clean. Again God was looking out for us.

What a gift He gave us with Reina living with us. Our house was small, and on the weekends, she had to sleep downstairs so Alyssa would have a place to sleep. Again, God knew our needs; we decided to buy a new house within a month. Reina was worried about where she would go. We told her we were moving to a four-bedroom house and she would have her own bedroom. Rick and I were honored to be asked to sit at Reina's parents' table at her wedding. Reina's parents have become good friends to us.

One day, Gina invited me and Rick to have dinner with her and her then boyfriend(Alan). I had a feeling they were going to announce their engagement, and I didn't want to go. After they announced their engagement, I told my friends about my concerns, and they listened but thought I was wrong. Gina never asked me my opinion, so I kept asking her if she was sure. What a place as a parent to be in. You hope you are wrong. Your child knows this person better than you. You can't say much because if you do, you might never see your child again.

While Reina was living with us, our daughter Gina, who had been married for about five months, was in a car accident and developed pancreatitis. That Thanksgiving, Gina was in the hospital in severe pain and unable to eat. Gina would spend three weeks in the hospital, hooked to an IV line. I spent a lot of time with her, but her husband only came when he felt like it. It was hard for me to see our child sick. Reina was a breath of fresh air for me. She became like a daughter to me. Again, God knew my needs. She would come in the house with a smile and would listen to my concerns.

I was so worried about Gina that I could not work one day after I was reassigned to pediatrics, not my usual unit. I broke down and started crying. I guess I was not as strong as I thought I was. It was hard seeing my child in pain. While visiting Gina one day, I said that I would trade places with her; she told me to go ahead, and we put our fists together to transfer places. I then told her that I knew from my mother's death that it would not be easy for her to watch me suffer.

One of the things Gina asked Alan to do before she came home was to clean the house. Later she told us that when she came home, everything was in such a mess that she wanted to go back to the hospital. Shortly after this, she took out a personal protection order against Alan, and he moved out. I always had concerns about their marriage. Gina then came to us to say that she was seeing Rich, who had a daughter, Brittany. Again a shock! We were angry, confused, and very upset.

Rick and I believed in permanent marriage, and we often worked with young couples to help them strengthen their marriages. Gina and Alan had made the Engaged Encounter. She later told us that he would not work on things and did not answer the questions.

Later, Gina would say that I was "into" the wedding. I told her that of course I would be into the wedding, as she was my only daughter, and one of the goals I had for my life was to give her a wedding. This was something we did not have; Rick and I paid for our own wedding. I wanted better things for our children.

While Gina's divorce was finalizing, I found I couldn't talk to her. I spent time at a program convention, running away from my daughter, crying and sharing my anger with a trusted friend. The irony was this friend had been divorced twice. My daughter knew that we would need time to process all of this, so we did not talk for several months. I had learned at this time in my life it's better not to talk than to say things I could not take back.

One of the things that came out in all of this was that her ex-husband (Alan) had gotten angry at his mother and needed a place to stay, so he moved in with Gina! Then she was trapped. She would have felt she had to go through with the marriage. I had fears because of her ex-husband's relationship with his mother. He did not treat his mother well. We did not even meet his mother till a day before the wedding. We did see her ex-husband one time after this to sort things out, but the marriage was over and our daughter was done. She later told us he had been verbally abusive. All in all, I was grateful she was no longer in an abusive marriage, but I really wished it hadn't happened this way.

At this time, Gina was singing in a choir. We had not yet met her new fellow. We went to two concerts where she was singing, and I had this strong sense that she was seeing this young, good-looking man. I watched both of them to get any clues. I saw none, but this feeling was there. When Gina introduced us to Rich, he was the man I had the feelings about. I greeted him with, "I knew it was you." Once again, God knew my needs.

My mother's sister Anne never married and lived in the house with my grandmother, Uncle Mike, and Aunt Mary (this was the house my mother took us to when she and my father separated). My grandmother and Aunt Mary died within a week of each other. So that left Uncle Mike and Aunt Anne living in the house. They lived together till my Uncle Mike died, and then Aunt Anne bought her sister and brothers out and stayed there. My mother would keep in touch with her. It was hard to be close to her, as she was very negative and opinionated. It was like she didn't know how to interact with people.

By this time, Aunt Anne had become what we now call a hoarder. But at the time we did know that there was a name for this. She would shop and buy many things, mostly things she didn't need. She also collected things. My mother saw it but never confronted her about it. My mother would say, "What are we going to do if something happens to her?" Of course, as it happened, it was my mother who died, and we had to take care of my aunt. I know this is awful to say, but at times I wished my aunt had died first. She was so difficult, no one (including me) wanted to be around her. She challenged me with the Bible verse from Matthew Matthew 5: 45(NIV): "If you love those who love you, what reward will you get? Are not even the tax collectors doing that? And if you greet only your brothers, what are you doing more than others? Do not even the pagans do that? Be perfect, therefore, as your heavenly Father is perfect." Because of my love for my mother, I felt she gave my aunt for me to help her. I chose to keep contact with my aunt.

From experience, I knew that she would not do well with family get-togethers. One time, she had my cousin pick her up on Christmas, but then she made him turn around and take her home. After my mother's death, once in awhile I would pick a day to visit her when I could spend all day doing what she wanted to do. We would shop where she wanted to go and eat at the restaurant of her choice. When I dropped her off back at the house, she never invited me inside, because it was such a mess. She was dirty, smelly, and unkempt.

Aunt Anne was a child of the Depression; she lived on a farm in rural Michigan in the 1920s. Her father died when she was eleven years old, and they never had much. The farm was sold when she was in her twenties, and she never got over that. After 9/11, I knew that she would not being doing well, but I chose not to visit her. I just couldn't seem to find the time.

One day, while I was at work, I received a call from the Detroit police, telling me that I needed to come and get my aunt. I wasn't sure what that meant. They told me that her neighbors had called them because she was confused and walking through the neighborhood, asking for water. The police had gone to her house, but she told them to leave. I was at work and would not be off for a few hours. I called my sister Mary to meet me at my aunt's house, not knowing what we would find. I thought maybe she would be dead. I was scared, so I called St. Rita's, the church she went to, and asked for help. One of the nuns who knew my aunt said that she would meet us at the house around 1830. None of us realized that it would be dark at that time, so we did not bring flashlights. When we knocked on her door, there was no response. We then called the police to help us get in the house. Mary went into the back door with the police.

They found my aunt barricaded in her bedroom. Mary kept calling out her name, and finally she came out with them. She looked relieved; her nightmare was over. We took her to the hospital, as she was dehydrated and looked like she had not eaten. There was only an old jar of mayonnaise in her refrigerator.

I agreed to become her guardian, and the next task was to clean out the house. I decided that a nursing home was the only place that Aunt Anne could live. We knew that she could never go back because she was unable to take care of herself. Our first idea was to take a match to all the stuff and walk away. Because my grandmother had lived in this house, we decided not to do that; also, we had heard that Aunt Anne's collection included a first edition Barbie.

I asked my brother and sister for help. This three-bedroom house, with a basement, was filled from floor to ceiling with stuff: paper, bags, mops, buckets, things from catalogs, cards, stamps, wooden furniture. There was no room to walk between boxes. The first day was the worst! We didn't know where to start. My son decided he would go into the basement, where he discovered a dead cat. He came up and vomited; the only way he went back down was with a mask. We also found mouse droppings. It was unbelievable that she was living like that.

After we cleaned that first day, I was covered in dirt from head to toe. I went home and showered and could not shower long enough. We kept plugging away at getting the house cleaned out. By the time we were done, we had filled six dumpsters full of stuff. We never found the old Barbie but we did find her sister, Skipper, in its original box; it sold for $500. My aunt never left the nursing home and she was never happy about that; she asked me one day if she could live with me.

After what we saw in the house, I knew that was not possible. I would always tell her I loved her, and one day she told me that she loved me. I only heard those words from her once in my life, but that was enough. What I learned and what God prepared me for was when I saw poverty and frail people, when I saw misery, I would not be afraid or avoid touching people because of what they looked like. I felt that if I could clean that house, I could do anything and go anywhere. I may not always like what I see. I would be careful to protect myself against illness and would not walk into filth, but I would do whatever God wanted me to do. Taking care of my aunt was just one of those things.

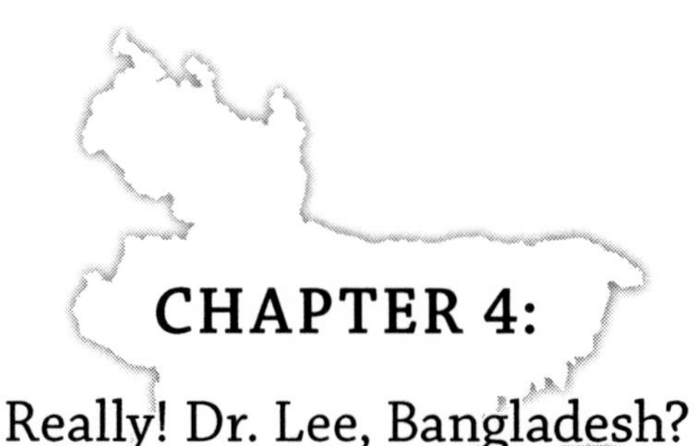

CHAPTER 4:

Really! Dr. Lee, Bangladesh?

Forget the former things; do not dwell on the past. See, I am doing new things! Now it springs up; do you not perceive it? I am making a way in the desert and streams in the wasteland. ISAIH 43:18-19(NIV)

The next part is my diary of my trips. I started writing my diary for Rick to read. I knew going abroad would be life changing, and I knew that sometimes when you go somewhere and try to explain to another person, you forget some things. I wanted Rick to share my experience. I'm glad I did, because I would have forgotten many experiences.

November 21, 2003

It's been about three weeks since I have known I'm going to Bangladesh. I am not sure I can spell it even. I can't believe I'm going. I've felt that God has put this in my heart for sometime. I remember when Gina was about six months old, I asked Rick to go with me to help some people overseas, but he was not interested. I was faced with going by myself and leaving my young daughter. I decided to stay with my husband and daughter. Life went on, and I have felt the calling again. I have been actively looking to go overseas as a nurse to help in foreign lands for two or three years. I asked Dr. Ventimigila at work and went to a meeting at his church, only to be told that because I didn't belong to his church, I couldn't go. I have been asking Dr. Rao to see if he knew of any opportunities. I even had two of my friends from work willing to go. But Dr. Rao said not this year.

Friends at work told me that Dr. Sang Lee goes overseas as an MD, so I went up to him and handed him my name and number. Dr. Lee called me the same day I went up to Dr. Ernie Mac and asked about going to the Philippines in January. Dr. Lee called me while my boss and friends were honoring Boss Day. I really couldn't believe it. When Dr. Lee said he was going in December, I was floored. So quickly! I would have to prepare, get shots, etc.

I am writing this about three weeks after finding out I'm going. I can't believe the way I am feeling. We had some good meetings with the Korean Methodist church. There are two MDs and two RNs going with four others. Dr. Lee keeps telling me that I'm going to the worst place for my first trip. We had several meetings and even went to dinner at the home of some people from Bangladesh. They are trying to teach me some words but language is hard for me. Dr. Lee' wife, Soo, is going, and she is just as sweet. Both of them give me such a warm feeling. Yesterday we packed up all the medicine and supplies to take. I felt useful and could determine what we should take. I must say today I'm a little scared. Joyce [a coworker] kept telling me to be careful and not be a hero. I have not thought of being a hero. Joyce doesn't know how afraid I am. I do feel like this is God's will for me. I have some lessons to learn. God! I will do your will always.

November 26, 2003

One week to go. I'm getting excited but nervous. I know it's God will for me to go but I'm anxious. Everyone keeps telling me how good I am for going, but I really don't want the praise. I just want them to look to themselves for ways to help people. We don't have to do great things. So far, only one person has offered me money. I feel sad about that. I'm sure the church could use the money. I still can't figure how I'm going to get all my clothes in a carry-on bag. Also I acted so badly about the possibility I will get my period. Then I remembered that women in that country get periods. I wonder what they do. I guess I'll find out.

December 1, 2003

Well, two days and counting. We went to the church for our send- off blessing. They showed a movie. That was the first time I got to see Bangladesh up close. I cried. What poverty. I feel so blessed but worry that we will not be able to help the people. The church people were so supportive; many came up to us and said that they would pray for us. Several people who had done a trip to Bangladesh talked to us. This reassured me that we will return. I am not feeling good. I think all the prescriptions I am taking are catching up with me. I have a headache and am nauseated most of the day. You would think the nausea would stop me from eating but it doesn't. My friends at work are supportive but only one person has offered me money. I am disappointed but maybe, after all, my friends just want to hear of my adventures, so I think God's plan is for them to hear from an eyewitness.

About Bangladesh

Bangladesh is one of the world's most densely populated countries. Its people are crammed into a delta of rivers that empty into the Bay of Bengal. Poverty is deep and widespread; almost half of the population lives on less than one dollar a day. The major employer is agriculture, but it is unable to provide enough jobs. Thus many Bengalis seek work abroad, often illegally.

Formerly East Pakistan, Bangladesh came into being only in 1971, when the two parts of Pakistan split after a bitter war that drew in neighboring India.

Concern has grown about religious extremism in the traditionally moderate country, which found apparent form in a string of bomb attacks in August 2005. The government has outlawed two fringe Islamic organizations.

Bangladesh has been criticized for its human rights record, with particular concern about assaults on women.

The low-lying country is vulnerable to flooding and

> cyclones, and it stands to be badly affected by predicted rises in sea levels.

The thing I never said in my diary was how I really only knew Dr. Lee as a coworker, but I didn't know him as well as some of the other doctors. Dr. Lee and I had worked together on a patient that was having chest pain, and I was impressed in what I saw, so when my coworker mentioned him, I thought I would give him a try. I handed Dr. Lee a piece of paper with my name and number and told him my skills. I was very excited when we talked and told him that this was something I thought I was called to do. I never gave it much thought, as I had been disappointed before. When Dr. Lee called me, I was so excited and couldn't believe I would being going. When we went to the Korean church for our first meeting, I was very overwhelmed and confused as to what we were going to do. Mrs. Yoo was at one of our meetings. She was going to Bangladesh to be an administrator there. I later learned that her husband had been shot and murdered in Detroit. She was trying to teach us Bengali for our trip. What was hard for me was she would say a word in Bengali and then translate it to Korean and then to English. Her English was not as good as her Korean. When we were packing up at the church, I was introduced to many Korean people, including Toots, another nurse, who was packing up most of the surgical supplies. I thought she was Korean, but that Sunday when I saw her at the Catholic church, I said to her, "I thought you were Korean." She laughed and said that she was Filipino. To this day we laugh about our first meeting. Toots has become one of my good friends. I am grateful God has put her in my life.

December 3, 2003

Well, the day is finally here. I had a rough day yesterday. My blood pressure has been up for about two weeks. Dr. Geimer has been treating me with medicine. Last Friday she added a second medicine. I haven't been feeling good since. I have been nauseated, dizzy, weak, and weak enough to need to lie down. I called her yesterday and she sent me to the lab for blood test and she told me to take one of the medicines away. How hard this is for her because I'm leaving and she worries about her patients. I will miss Rick. We spent last night together after Bible study.

December 3, 2003, 1045

We are at the airport. Everything went well at the baggage check in. We had to pay for extra luggage, but the church picked up the charges. I have said good-bye to Rick already. He had been so supportive. I could see he was a little nervous but is happy for me. The prayer service was meaningful, both in Korean and English. It means so much that people are praying for us. We could not be doing this without their love and support of many people. How loved I am. Thank you, God.

December 4, 2003

This has been a long plane ride. We have been flying for eleven hours. I rested but couldn't sleep. This is a growing experience. This plane is huge: sixty rows with ten seat across. We have had dinner and a snack, and we will be getting breakfast. We sure don't go hungry. It was wonderful to see the Baltic Sea. Nothing but snow and water. I never thought I would be doing such a thing.

December 5, 2003

We are now on our way to Dhaka, Bangladesh. We arrived in Bannock, Thailand, around midnight. I finally meet Connie Escrupolo. She is so nice. I really like her. What I could see of Bannock, it was busy. It smelled bad. It reminded me of coming in from down south off I-75. Our cab driver was driving so fast, he scared Soo. Our hotel is nice, with beautiful floors of marble. I was able to take some pictures of a shrine. We will be in Dhaka in just a few minutes. I will write later.

December 5, 2003, 1430

I am sitting in the compound, enjoying a peaceful moment. We made it. The airport was hard. While we were waiting for our passports, I could see and feel the sadness of the people. Most of the men in line had such sadness in their eyes. I could see some fighting while we waited. It looked like they were being sent back to the end of the line. They were not happy about that. The border guard tried to stop us from bringing in supplies. Mr. Song got stopped first. I don't know if this was because he was Korean or because of the bags. Connie ran and got through. I'm slow and got stopped too. My heart was racing and I kept on walking and praying. They kept questioning us. They wanted money and tax. I wouldn't mind that if the tax would help the people, but I have the feeling it would help them get rich. We are in the hotel. Our driver Gabriel was nice but did not understand us. I met Peter and Sarah, two of our team members who have just come from Thailand and are sick. She shared how she had diarrhea for a day. This is just a reminder how careful I must be.

I can see the poverty at every turn. The water is very dirty. Everyone seems to have their own home, all over Dhaka, with all types of clothing hanging out. I was taking some pictures. I noticed the children. My heart is with the children. I waved and took some pictures and they waved back. They were playing and waved and called me "sister." I noticed a young woman looking up at me and smiling. The children smiled, and I have a feeling if I would have stayed here long we would have been friends. I do feel strange as a white woman here and must remember as a woman and a Christian to smile and let them see God's love.

I feel safe here at this compound but find myself crying at what I see. We are sitting here looking out the window, watching people. We have been watching this man watering what seems to be his field. We keep laughing and watching how hard he works. He's carrying two buckets and a pan and sprinkling water on the field. He finishes his pail and then goes to get more water. We [Connie and Soo and I] have a laugh and talk about our experience. Here we sit as women from Korea, America, and the Philippines. We discuss our common faith and shared experiences but also what the women we see here might be going through. I keep noticing a woman in red; she seems to be picking weeds. I suppose these are for dinner. I notice the Muslim prayers over the loudspeaker. I wanted to hear them from the outside but it was too late. I can't imagine the chants all day long.

We are all together. Dr. Mehta and Nikki have arrived. They both look tired. We are just sitting and talking. Watching TV—imagine that?

December 5, 2003, 2020

I keep challenging myself. I don't know if I'm stupid or just naïve. I went out of the complex with Dr. Mehta and Nikki. I was scared. There were so many people out on the street. I knew that I was white and a woman and different. I hope this did not challenge our being here. The poverty was worse than I imagined, many men on the street, men sitting by fires, talking, trying to sell things. I was very afraid. I was afraid that we were being followed to be robbed. I only saw a few women, one was very skinny. I also saw a family by the fire: husband, wife, and a child. I saw the hopelessness in her eyes. We passed a dumpster with garbage: what a smell. What am I doing here? God, what do you want of me? Must I tell what I've seen? How can I explain what I see in their faces? I am afraid to make eye contact. I know I will be judged by my actions. What I do as a Christian and what I do as a white woman. Soo tells me I have curiosity. She says I am very curious. I guess I never though of myself that way. I reflect that this is a good trait.

We met the director, Chang Soon Hong. This man is amazing. He is a Korean who has lived in Bangladesh for twenty years. He told us last night that he did not want to come here. He wanted to be in Tibet. His family did not want him to come here. But he found his purpose here. He says he loves the people. Soo told us that his wife lives in the United States with their children. His wife works in a doctor's office. Soo also said that Director Chang has been sick twice with dengue fever. I could tell he has a terrible cough.

When I read this now some eight years later, I see that I did not do a good job of explaining what this first trip was like, especially the first time I entered Bangladesh. It was during the day, and I could see the sun through the window at customs, but I was overwhelmed with feelings of sadness, profound sadness. I felt this in my spirit before I left customs. I turned to Soo and told her that I felt the sadness in my spirit, and she agreed. The line to go through customs was long and slow. There was no trying to make things easier for anyone, even the locals. The Bangladesh people seemed to get a rough time by the officials. When we left customs, we were told to go quickly, find our bags, and leave immigration as fast as we could. I had a hard time finding my assigned bag with medical supplies, and Mr. Song, knowing it was my first trip and being the gentleman he is, was trying to help me. I think when the officials noticed us together with these big bags, they knew something was up. That is why we were stopped. The officials told me to stop and I don't know what I was thinking, but I kept walking. I am not the type of person who would not obey authority. Mr. Sang had brought a sewing machine for the people at the school. The officials gave him a hard time about this and wanted him to pay to bring it into Bangladesh. Mr. Song told them he would not pay and would leave the machine at the airport to be picked up by us when we were leaving Bangladesh. The officials let us go after a while.

Then there was the scene at the airport. I was overwhelmed by what I saw. We trying to get into the van, and across the street was a fence with people on the other side, begging. The sadness was everywhere. Their hands were reaching through the fence, and the sound was something I will never forget. Once in the van, we were on the street and I was again overwhelmed by the traffic. There were lane markers, but no one followed any order. I saw no traffic lights. The traffic was vans, busses with people riding on top, rickshaw bikes, and pedestrians. The drivers used no turn signs, just honked their horns and went.

When we got to the hotel where we would spend the night, I was relieved to see that it was one international travelers used. The hotel reminded me of a dorm room. We were up on the third floor and had to carry our bags up the stairs. Connie and I shared a room. We had some down time, so Connie, Soo, and I got to know each other better.

The thing about the man watering his field with a bucket was that we watched him repeat a simple task and saw how he could have done it quicker and with less work. We had a laugh at watching him. Also the children waving to us were squatters (people who make their home wherever there is open land); it was difficult for me to see children living like this. Connie sang hymns in our room with joy. When she and I talked, she shared that Bangladesh was not her choice for where she wanted to do service work. This was her second time here. She had been on other missions with Dr. Lee, and he asked her to go to Bangladesh with him again.

Going out on the street, I found myself fearful. Even though I had been out on the streets of Detroit at night, I was scared on the street in Bangladesh. Dr. Mehta sensed my fear and told me the people would not hurt me; they were curious about me, but I felt defenseless. After sensing my fear, Nikki and Dr. Mehta walked me back to the compound and kept walking.

December 6, 2003

I woke up at 0130 and then again at 0415. Connie was up also, so we showered and started to talk. I find the 0500 chants hard; you hear this moaning (praying). I tried to leave the building to listen outside but the gate door was closed. I can't imagine hearing this every morning. Dr. Mehta, Nikki, and Peter went for a run this morning; they came back soaking wet. We did morning exercise. Dr. Lee gave me a book on Bangladesh, so I started reading it. We will be eating breakfast soon, and then taking a plane up to see the people. I really like being with these people [the people in our group]. I'm learning so much about life.

December 6, 2003, 1130

We have been on the road for a while. We are sitting at the airport, waiting to catch a plane to Saenoon. [This is a school in Bangladesh sponsored by Chilmary Medical Center.] As soon as we got out of the van, the children kept saying, "Good morning, madam." They surrounded me first. They smiled and bowed. There seemed to be joy among them. We sat in on the teachers' meeting and met the teachers. Two Korean teachers were beautiful women with much joy in their faces. There were several Indian [Bangladesh] teachers. We met the computer teacher. He seemed nervous;

I sensed that he wanted to make a good impression. We went into the sewing room. They had old Singers there. I had not seen these machines except at my grandmother's. I saw patterns that were old. The school was old and looked like there were no supplies. The computer room at least had newer supplies. The building was old. The children started the morning with a song and a prayer. They stood in line and were well behaved. I still noticed the stares. I kept my sunglass off so that I could see their eyes and they could see mine.

Then we went back on the street. I got to sit in the front because of my size. I had to buckle up or my fears would get the best of me. There seems to be no order to traffic here. We walk the streets of Bangladesh. What an experience, people everywhere. Lots of shops: hanging meat, chicken, fresh fruit. Once again the children follow us. They are looking at all of us but have a fascination with me. We walk a narrow path through their homes (shacks), one on top of another. We walk through water. Women look out at us. What must these people think of us? I hope they know this is not a show. What had caused this madness? What resources does this country have that have yet to be found?

When I read what I wrote, I can see my anger at the end of my writing. We went through a squatters' village. This was one of the poor areas in Bangladesh. The shacks were made of old wood, cardboard, and whatever people could find. A family would live in these shacks. Inside you would see a pot above a fire and no running water. When I look at what we have and what they have, it breaks my heart for my fellow men, women, and children. We are so blessed. I can't pretend I did not see these people. To this day, I am haunted and changed by what I saw.

Mr. Chang is such a good man. He makes sure we have rolls of toilet paper for the trip. I keep hearing his cough. I sense he is not healthy. What makes him choose to live here? We go to the Dhaka Music School. He was able to start this school with the government's help. We met the teachers and saw the piano practice rooms and the instrument rooms. This building is beautiful, and we pass guards, as we always do. We go back out on the street. What happened next was told to me by Soo, as I was in the front seat and didn't see what happened. A beggar approached our bus; he was skinny and known to Director Chang. What they said happened next is the director pulled the man's earnings [from begging] out of his pocket and said, "Not bad," and that he should eat more. Soo and Connie laughed so hard about this. He told them that this man was new to begging. We headed for the airport. More confusion, sitting in uncomfortable chairs. We talk again and share with Mrs. Kim; she is such a gentle person, and I just love her. She is a teacher and was very excited when I told her my daughter is a music teacher. God works in strange ways; while at the airport, Connie finds some Filipino people. They share, and guess what? They are internal medicine doctors, working about sixty minutes from where we will be. They want us to come see them. They are looking for an OB doctor. We are all excited. We are thousands of miles from home, and we meet. We tease Connie about wanting to go to Mongolia instead of here. Connie had been with Dr. Lee once here and really didn't like this place. Why am I here? I hope it's not just to tell this story.

We are on the plane to Chilmary. This plane is small. We like Thai Air better. Nikki is tired and showing signs of wear. She is so cute, and it's been good for her to be with her father. The plane is filled with people. I have the feeling I can't get any bigger or I won't fit in the seats.

I must backtrack and tell you a joke between Soo, Connie, and myself. Connie, Philip, and I were walking outside on the street the first day. I asked Philip what this beautiful building across the street was. He told me it was a community center, and then he told me the next building was a "bang" house. Connie thought he said "bank," but I took it to mean a whorehouse. We have been watching this building a lot, and it has been a private joke between us.

I really like these people. I'm starting to miss Rick. I wonder how things are at home, but once again, I'm glad I came.

December 6, 2003, 1815

We arrive at dark. Well, what a bus ride. I thought driving in LA was bad, but the three hours we just spent in a bus [van] was bad! You meet bikes, rickshaws, oxen, and wagons. We went through so many towns, villages, so many people. Three of us (Nikki, Dr. Mehta, and a Korean man we met at the airport) were in a van. Nikki and Dr. Mehta slept most of the trip. I prayed and committed my life to God and Jesus. I did some soul searching and remembered the Beatitudes. How blessed I am. I hope I can remember these lessons. I keep looking at these people with curiosity; Soo is right. I wonder how these people came here. I can't imagine staying here, and the selfish part of me wants to go home. What have I done, and why am I here? The sleeping area is okay, and Director Chang is embarrassed because we have a trunk(from the compound with their supplies) in our room; he has it removed and it is better. Soo, Connie, Dr. Lee, Nikki, and Dr. Mehta share stories about our ride. Soo tells us about her driver and his impatience. He would put the siren on. We laugh and tease Connie about coming back twice, but under the laughter is profound gratitude at our lives.

December 6, 2003, 2200

We met each other and ate dinner with our hands, India [Bengal] food. The schedule was explained. I'm grateful for the food and how attentive and loving they are to us. Two Korean women, Miss Chang and Ms. Rhu (Sue He), really look forward to us coming. Also the people look forward to our coming. They must see our Christian beliefs. Meeting the people without crying for me will be hard. I keep seeing the hopelessness in their eyes. I can't believe people ride on top of busses. I wonder how many die. We set up the OR. We could use more supplies. We brought two bags of food for the people staying here. Director Chang said he brought a TV with satellite to help Sue He or she will burn out. I could really understand that.

December 7, 2003, 0830

We are starting soon. Last night was hard. I kept hearing all the noises. I slept for hours and then woke up. The birds made a terrible sound. I also felt Satan trying his tricks. I was able to cast him out. I felt so sick from the medicine but have to take in breakfast.

December 7, 2003, 2000

I am so tired. I was up so early and worked so hard. What a day! We did nine cases, two modified hysterectomies, and several tumor removals. What confusion! The local police were out in force for crowd control. Good, I think we needed it. We had crowds of people to see. They came because of the GYN. We saw many prolapes, some yeast infections, some infertility cases. At first there was chaos but we did get our rhythm. We had several local helpers. The OR local helper was good. It was hard because of the need for translation. The first case we did was on a woman that was so scared. I spent a lot of time comforting her. The women here are so modest. I cannot even open their legs to check them, let alone Dr. Lee.

We meet some challenges. The Bangladesh people don't trust me. I don't know if they have ever seen a white woman. The second woman, while scared, was a model patient. We had to move the patient to a recovery room, an agriculture center. The first woman had a terrible recovery (she seemed to need a lot of attention). Her daughter was with her, and she vomited. Miss Chang is with me. She is so gentle. We need to pray for all three of these people, who stay and devote their lives to helping others, as their work is so hard. I am leading prayers in the morning, so I met with Gabriel; he will be my translator. I never had a translator before. The people here seem to have a sparkle.

We met with the staff in the morning. We saw the children. How I love their faces. They sang for us. Music is the universal language of love. I miss the children. We are getting along well. We laugh a lot. People in our house are having a lot of fun with each other. Hope I can sleep tonight. I hear people singing. I just hate hearing the loud prayers every morning.

I still remember it like it was yesterday. We were in a room with the workers of the Chilmary Medical Center compound. Men and women, teachers, and workers were doing morning devotions, reading from the

Bible and singing. The people led the devotions. Just before I spoke, we sang "How Great Thou Art." I started to cry. I couldn't believe I was here sharing this moment. We were singing this song in our native tongue. Americans, Koreans, Bangladesh, and Filipino. I can still go back to this memory. Every time I hear or sing "How Great Thou Art," I go back to that memory This was something I felt God called me to but I never really thought this moment would come. I still remember Dr. Lee with the tambourine. Dr. Lee is a great surgeon but music is not his thing; his joy in playing makes up for that. To see his face and that joy is hard to describe. I spoke that day but really don't know what I said. It was different through translation. Gabriel had asked me to tell him some of my story the day before because he knew British English, not American English, and he was having a hard time with translation. I really never knew how skilled he was in translating.

December 9, 2003, 1800

I remember that it's my mother's birthday. We worked hard. We did eight surgery cases. Mostly "lumps and bumps," as Dr. Mehta calls them. Dr. Mehta did the surgeries. Dr. Lee took over. We are starting to run out of everything. No more sterile gowns. Working conditions are hard. We have two lights hanging from a string. I almost caused a disaster. The light was around a fan, and guess what I did? I turned on the fan. We had a lady who needed a prolapes repair. She stayed overnight for vomiting and continued to vomit in the morning. We started an IV and tried to keep track of her, but we were so busy with the OR that we had to hurry to go to the island before dark. I had to go to the bathroom, therefore was rushed. When we got on the boat, I thought of her. No one knew if she had left; we had visions of her still being hooked up to IV (dry by now), unable to go to the bathroom. We laughed so hard, we imagined her still hooked to an IV. Thank God someone looked after her. It must have been a local nurse.

What lessons I've learned. One of the things that has been hard on me is the food. Rice with every meal, spicy vegetables, fish, and we had beef tonight. We eat seaweed in the evening. I'm enjoying rice wrapped with seaweed. We went to the island after work. What a beautiful and peaceful place.

Fresh water. We went on a motorized boat. We sat on the top of the roof and enjoyed the view. I was scared of getting on top of the roof. My fears came out. I kept looking for life jackets and thought about our safety; what if the boat tipped? We would drown. I also got my period today early. I was hoping I would not get it till we got to Thailand. I guess I get to see what the women go through here.

It's been a rough day and a blessed day. I spoke in front of the group in the morning. I said the things I planned but forgot to talk about diversity. Maybe God wanted a short message, as I just went blank. We sang "How Great Thou Art," one of my favorite hymns. When the six of us are together, we laugh a lot. We seem to get along well. One of the things I haven't mentioned is that we eat with our fingers. Our fingers turn yellow from all the seasonings. Also about the showers: pouring warm water over the head. Felt good the first day, but today my water was cold. One of the nine-year-old girls we did OR on today had an extra digit on her finger . She had to wait till she was nine to have this removed; in America, this would have been done within her first year of life.

I was so exhausted, I stepped on a puppy. We have four puppies on the grounds. I'm missing Rick.

December 9, 2003

One of the things I found interesting was in one of the buildings where we are staying, Director Chang had a satellite dish. He felt that one of the administrators was having a hard time so he thought the TV would help. Some things about the buildings: we have several buildings. We have a bathroom with a shower but ours is cold. Soo's shower is just a faucet; you fill a pan and pour water over your head. I took a shower in Soo's bathroom with cold water. We do have electricity with fans but they are old.

December 9, 2003, 1815

Well, the day is over. We finished OR at 1600. We are getting tired. It's has been so confusing. We are starting to get tired, all of us. The emotions

I feel with these people (our group) is strong. We pray and have tea three times a day, and we laugh with each other. Today we had to turn down several people as far as doing their surgery. It was so hard to choose one over another. The wife of the man who served us dinner needed hand surgery, but Dr. Mehta turned her down. I could tell by his eyes how hurt he was. He must love his wife a lot. That has been the hardest part of the trip. How do you choose? Dr. Mehta is feeling it too. I could tell he wanted to help everyone. He is quite gifted. We are so limited because no gas, no good local(anesthesia) . He said several times he could help these people but did not have the right equipment.

Dr. Lee saw mostly medical people. We were going to the market by rickshaw. I was very scared but because of my period, I didn't feel I could enjoy the time in the market. I also don't think I can take the poverty again, no running toilets, cooking by fire. Outside the complex haunts me. I feel safe inside. The people that work here have a better life. The farming school is working. I'm starting to eat the food more but still so much rice. I didn't go with others to the market. I walked back to our house and starting writing and then started crying. What was I supposed to learn here? Why did I come? I don't know if my being here made any difference.

Nikki had a great time with the children. I so wanted to use my pediatrics skill but without anesthesia, neither doctor wanted to operate on children. We did operate on a ten-year-old child with a growth on her buttocks. She was pretty. The $100 Geri Flannery gave me I gave away; we don't need the money. The last few years God had blessed us so. I remember telling Rick I would give his money away. Director Chang has a great program here, and he is such a good man, a saint. He has thought so many things through. He told us that the money we all gave would go for the workers' Christmas party. I have made some friends here. Two of the nurses asked me if I would come back. They were trying to teach me some of their language. I told them God willing I will try to come back. It will be hard to leave tomorrow but I want to go home. I want to see Rick, talk to Mark and Gina, and see my friends at work. We are laughing again because I didn't ride the rickshaw, but I am the only one who has a picture.

I remember these things like it was yesterday. I had come back from lunch before everyone. We had turned the fan off for lunch. I went back into our OR and turned the switch for the fan, not seeing that the lamp cord was around the fan. I was so scared. I really could have caused a disaster. One of the things I never did in nursing was to work as a circulator in the OR. The circulator is responsible for keeping everything moving. They are a go-for. They run for instruments if they fall on the floor or get something the surgeon needs that was not put out; they put out more sponges if need, help gown the surgeon, adjust the lights if needed, put out sutures, do a surgical scrub if needed, make sure everything that is needed in the OR is there. The scrub tech or nurse hands instruments to the doctor and is sterile. The circulator is not sterile but can't break sterile technique. Because of working in OB, I would go into OR for C-sections to catch the baby (the term we use for the nurse who took care of the baby). I started getting comfortable in the OR. As a student I had been in the OR only one or twice, we did not have a rotation through OR, so it was a foreign land to me. I was very challenged here and was grateful that I had two doctors who knew that and had patience with me.

The local nurses were not very friendly at first; it was like we had invaded their space. I also didn't feel very good, especially after I got my period. I had a history of very heavy periods, lots of bleeding. It also didn't help that the bathroom Connie and I shared with Nikki and Dr. Mehta did not have a flush toilet. We would have to put water into a pan and pour it down the toilet till the waste went down. Once again God had prepared me, as pouring water down the toilet to flush was something I had to do as a child in my home.

I was so embarrassed and overwhelmed. Most of us medical people can become embarrassed if we are working closely with people and they become our friends and we have to share personal information. I had a very hard time on top of the boat, worrying about bleeding on my clothes, and that is why I didn't go to the market. When I was able to relax, sitting on top of the boat, I was able to see the beauty of Bangladesh. When I wrote about crying when I was alone, I was sobbing. I was emotionally exhausted. I had dreams of doing so much;

what we did helped a few, but there was so much more to do. Our trip to the island was a real eye opener for me. The island was green and peaceful. These islands were called by Director Chang "disappearing islands," and he would joke about selling us one of them. We walked on the island for some time and then came to a few straw huts. We met the owners of the huts, who were friendly; they allowed us to look inside their huts and take pictures of them. It was so hard for me to believe people lived like this in this century. These people would have to find other places to live when the floods came or they would drown.

December 10, 2003, 0705

We are leaving soon. We are packing up now. I woke up at 0300 but then slept till 0500; my period woke me up. I find myself emotional this morning; I am eager to get home but the faces of the people will be in my heart. This morning is cloudy but warm. I wake up with the morning prayers. I have received compliments because I have been able to adapt well. Dr. Lee and Soo stayed up till 0200, talking with Madame Yoo. She is getting discouraged. I did not know she was married; her husband was murdered in Detroit. She has grown children. What a challenge she has, doing this work. I forgot to tell you about the dog; she has three puppies: black, white, and mixed. I can tell she wants to wean them but they still want mother's milk. I stepped on one, and boy did she scream. I feel safe with the dogs.

I was scared in the van on the ride home. I had just taken a car seat safety class and became a child restraint technician. While taking this class, I had to learn about crashes, impact, and injuries from crashes. Because of my size I was in the front seat, not a good place for someone without a seat belt after taking that class. I asked Dr. Mehta to change places with me, this helped, along with keeping my eyes closed some of the trip.

December 10, 2003, 1930

We are back in Dhaka. We left around 0930 after morning prayers and singing. It was hard to leave, to leave Madame Yoo and Madame Chang. Hope they can stay there. It was hard to leave the people we met, the nurses, Dr. Russell, Gabriel (my translator), the man that served us dinner. I hug all of them. I don't know if it was proper for me to hug a man but I did. I was spontaneous but forgot where I was. What must they think? We went to the leprosy center. What a dream.

We are driving again. What a challenge. It's a wonder people don't die. Nikki says that her brother should come here if he wants to play video games. We have so many near misses. They honk their horns all the time to try to go faster. The ride is hard. We are tight in the car. Nikki and I have room but because the road is so rough, it's hard on the muscles. I close my eyes a good amount of the time. I keep looking out to see the people and their way of life. We see a few gas stations. We passed a brick making town. Every few miles there is another market. Lots of peoples, many sitting around; I see someone playing chess.

We ate at a Chinese restaurant. The food is better than the food I have been eating. The chicken has curry but is small. We had egg drop soup with vinegar and hot peppers. It feels good to have soup; I have missed it. We went shopping at Aragon. Director Chang looked pleased as we buy something. I buy some purses and a leather wallet for Rick, and book for Alyssa, a purse for Gina and a gold boat for myself. I forgot Mark. Well, I will try in Thailand. On our plane ride to Dhaka, I sat with someone from CARE. She wanted to talk but I was so tired. I did take her card and gave it to Director Chang. I apologized for being tired. She told me that the prime minister's sister was on the plane. She is the minister of women and children. Dhaka looks different to me this time. We go past the American and Korean embassy; they are across the street from each other. We went to the nice area of Bangladesh. The traffic is wall-to-wall people. We pass a bus, and if I reach my hand out, we could touch each other. Mrs. Kim is tired; she has been traveling for a month. She says she will have her family home for Christmas. It's hard to see it as Christmas. It is warm here; we are wearing short sleeves and running fans. I have enjoyed seeing the flowers. I smell the roses.

We are in the Chilmary Medical Center facility in Dhaka. Overhead we keep hearing helicopters. They fly over five or six times. I keep thinking it's for us, but really we are not that important. We hear that there was a shooting on the street yesterday. Well, now I know my fears were real. Having my period has made me very nervous. I keep going to the bathroom. Everyone is noticing. I can't help it, it feels like I'm hemorrhaging. We have dinner: chicken, cabbage, rice, and cucumbers. We heard that Afghanistan was bombed. We have lost all track of time and events. We are in a time warp. I am glad we are going home. Soo says that there has been some tension between Korea and Bangladesh. Dr. Mehta embarrassed Nikki. The teachers from the Korean school were being teased about finding a husband. Dr. Mehta brings out the homecoming pictures of the boys and tells them to pick one. We laughed so hard and then Director Chang put his finger on Nikki's boyfriend. She is so embarrassed but loves this. Nikki is so cute. We have talked a lot. I think she misses her mother. We sit watching a soccer game on TV. Everyone is talking in Korean. I forgot what we had for lunch but I had my first coke in a week.

Sometimes the air really smelled; Director Chang says that people are drying fish. On our trip we passed rice patties; the people were drying rice on the road, fanning the rice. With cars on the road, how clean is this? This experience has helped me imagine what it must have been like in Jesus' time (minus the cars). Most of the cars are old and foreign. The rickshaws are also old. We see people carrying old baskets and logs on carts; there are wagons with oxygen. The ground is so sandy, and water is red, green, and black. We went over this old wood bridge where only one car could pass at a time. That water looked clean.

When I read my words now, I see that I really didn't explain what happened to me on the road going home in Bangladesh. I always wanted to go to Jerusalem, to walk where Jesus walked, I guess, hoping to find Jesus. But in that van, looking out the window in Bangladesh, I found Jesus as I passed the villages and saw how the people dressed: the women with their heads covered (looking like Mary, Jesus' mother, might look), some men with skirts instead of pants, scarves around their necks, most unshaved with beards. The people had sandals on their feet. I saw buildings made out of anything available: cardboard, wood, metal, bricks. I saw businesses close to the road. As we passed through the many towns and villages, I would see the people doing all kinds of trade. I would see people talking with each other. We would pass many markets with food, fruits, chickens, rice, and staples needed to survive. I did a lot of soul searching while I was on that road. Why did I suffer with such self-pity when I lived in the United States? What I saw there in my mind had not progressed except the cars in centuries. I also did wrestle with all these people; why not abort the poor? I looked out the window and saw people suffering and I wondered what Jesus would think and wonder if he would see that nothing has changed, people are still suffering, and we are not doing what he tried to show us: to love our neighbor as ourselves. What really hit me was looking at the ground ,mostly flat land; we would see fields of mostly rice, the trees were mostly bamboo, we were traveling on two-lane dirt roads. Most of the trees were covered with dirt. We would meet oxen carrying heavy loads of wood behind them. I wrestled with many things on that trip; in the end, I found Jesus and recommitted my life, my dreams, my hopes, and my will to him. I never expected to find him in Bangladesh. I knew that God would want me to come back to Bangladesh, and I was not sure that I wanted to. My intention was to help people, not get anything for myself. I did pray the sinner's prayer on that trip. I did write for the Korean Methodist church paper and spoke about this publicly after we returned.

December 11, 2003, 0600

I am awake early again, but I feel more rested. It was by my standards a quiet night in the city. I'm showered and in a dress. I'm tired of tennis shoes; my feet feel so tight in them. We have covered so much of the world. I never dreamed I would do this, or maybe I did and that is why I'm here. I can't wait for the debriefing meeting. It will be nice to share; we have been so close as a group. I am more positive and have fewer complaints. I realize how negative I have been. The Bangladesh women are so sad; their eyes are sad; they have had a hard life. We didn't have much time to talk about God; I hope we showed our Christianity. I will never forget devotions. Dr. Lee, Soo, Mr. Song, and Peter were talking about their church vision. I have my thoughts but I'm an outsider and don't know enough. I think they need to follow the Acts of the Apostles for guidance. They are so devoted to the church and helping others.

December 11, 2003, 1400

We are finally on the plane going to Thailand, going home. It will be a long process. We got to look at Dhaka for one last time. We had devotions with the staff at Chilmary Medical Center and Director Chang. Dr. Lee gave a moving explanation of Islam and Christianity. Dr. Lee is a good and faithful man. We had a close-out meeting. We were all moved. I was quite emotional. I will miss being with Dr. Mehta and Nikki; God, please give them a save trip home. We were able to go through special roads that are better. There are still so many people. Dr. Lee and I got to talk alone and shared some personal things. I hope I'm able to share with my friends all the things I have learned. I hope when I am tempted to complain, I will think of Bangladesh and what people there go through. Two beggars stop at our window (in the van) and look for money. This is so hard but I know if I give them money, I will be attacked. It is better I give my money to programs than to individuals; I can help many more people. I am glad I did not look up Skihoom; we are in Thailand such a short time that it would have just disrupted his life.

Skihoom was a young man that we sponsored from the time he was five years old; he was twenty years old at this time. The last letter we got from him, he wrote that if we ever came to Thailand to look him up. He said that he would be our tour guide.

December 12, 2003

We spent the night in Thailand. We arrived around 1900. We went to our room, had dinner, and talked. We ate seafood: lobster (the largest I've ever seen), shrimp, spicy soup, squids, clams, and more. It was expensive, over $400. I felt bad but enjoyed the meal and the company. Connie also enjoyed herself. We were too late for shopping. I needed to buy some sanitary pads. I was able to find my way around the store (looked like Meijers) and find the pads. I guess I am a world traveler.

The store was very large; I was embarrassed to being buying sanitary pads, so I went off by myself. I laugh as I think of how I found where they kept the pads. I tried asking a saleswoman who did not speak English, she call another saleswoman, who did not speak English; the next thing I knew I had several saleswomen trying to understand me. I ended up pointing to my bottom for understanding; finally someone knew what I needed and I was able to find the pads. I ended up charging this, as I had no Thai money. As I was checking out, Mr. Song was there, making sure I was safe, and this only added to my embarrassment.

My leg has been cramping since I woke up, and I'm in a lot of pain. I walking but slowing everyone up. They are so patient with me and concerned. I really like being with these people. Mr. Song is upset at the bill. They charged us for ice. I laugh because I'm the only one who doesn't want ice. They gave us a wet hand towel and charged us for this. Mr. Song has traveled a lot and never saw this. Connie and I talk for a little while. I'm tired, so we share our thoughts. She will be lonely without us, but she has been single by choice, she has helped her family. She is upset because some of her nieces just want to have babies. She says this will be the first year her family will be together. Now that Connie has left, I'm the only one that doesn't speak Korean. I'm amazed how people can speak so many languages; I have trouble with English. My thoughts today are happy that I had this experience. It has been a hard experience on me physically but spiritually wonderful. I keep hearing the hymns. I hope God blesses me with another trip. I'm not sure I want to go back to Bangladesh, but if God calls me I will go. Thank you, God, I praise you!

Connie was in the Philippines, and we met in Thailand, so she flew back to the Philippines from Thailand.

December 12, 2003

I can see the ground. We are making our descent home. It's been a long trip. I was very tired. I was glad because I had an exit seat for the trip home, but then this big tall man sat next to me; I'm in the middle. I can't move and I'm feeling sick. Mr. Kim comes to visit, and I discover they have no one sitting between them. I ask Paul to change seats with me, and he does. What a gift of love. I'm able to sleep for about an hour; I feel refreshed, and I'm able to go on. The sun is coming through the window; the temperature outside is 28°F; in Bangladesh, it was 80°F. It will take me some time to get used to this coldness. Thank you, God, for your many gifts.

CHAPTER 5:

Really, Dr. Mac! The Philippines?

January 13, 2006

Well, it's been two years since I wrote in this journal. I was really changed when I came back from my trip. I had seen things most people don't see. I tried to tell people about the experience, but really, how can I describe it? Most people don't understand. I don't blame them; how could they? We are all in our own little world. I'm still working in OB-post partum. I enjoy the work but know God has plans for me. I have seen my daughter married and divorced and remarried, all within two years. Five months after her first marriage, she developed pancreatitis, and her husband was not supportive. He just didn't understand, nor did he want to change. Because of my beliefs, her divorce was hard on me. I keep learning life's lessons, sometimes the hard way. I have been in Bible study for three years now. I am learning so much. We are studying Revelation. I feel very blessed. I have a good job, a good husband, a nice home, and good friends.

I am on my way to the Philippines with Dr. Mac. I have been so excited but have been having some medical issues. I have been taking malaria medicine for two weeks. The day before I left, my blood pressure went up and I felt sick. I'm still feeling a little headache right now. My leg has been hurting off and on from exercise; only Motrin and rest helps. Last night I went to the bathroom, stepped the wrong way, and felt intense pain. I thought, There goes the trip. I couldn't get out of bed. I'm still feeling pain, but taking Motrin and rest helps. I have met some of the people on the trip with me;

they are a lot of fun. I met Dr. Peter, Sarah and Jane (both RNs), and Dr. Mike. I am sitting next to two nice people; this will make the trip go faster. I feel very upbeat though not physical well. I will be going to Bangladesh (God willing) three weeks after I come back. Dr. Lee said people saw my compassion and asked for me to come back. How could I say no? Rick is so supportive. I know he worries; I love him. I am counting on God to give me the strength, as I know my family still need me.

I would later learn that I had torn a ligament in my knee. My doctor, Dr. Geimer, was very angry that I did not call her before I left. When we landed in Manila, my first impression of the Philippines was much different than Bangladesh. As we were exiting the plane, we heard Filipino music; there was a band greeting us. I was given a lei with Sampaguita, the flower of the Philippines. The flower smelled so good. Next Dr. Mac had arranged for me to go through the customs line for dignitaries. We then were greeted by her sister-in-law and taken to our hotel. I meet Lori, a Filipino woman, there; she would be my roommate. She went to St. Anastasia, the church I attended, and my friend had arranged for me to room with her. I was grateful as I did not want to stay alone.

We woke up early and went to breakfast in our hotel, and as I was sitting there eating, over walked Carla, who worked at the same hospital as me in Michigan! She said, "What are you doing here?" I explained that I was here with PMA (Philippines Medical Association of Michigan) to do medical and surgical work. We were both so shocked; neither of us knew we would be going on this journey. She had missed the meeting we had before we left. Seeing her there was a blessing, as Carla and I have shared some wonderful talks many times.

We were told to be on time for the bus, not Filipino time (late). The bus ride was fun. A big coach bus, not a van.

January 14, 2006

Well, I'm in the Philippines. What a day. We left late at 0800, two bus loads. The country looks better than Bangladesh, more beautiful. We see some mountains. We drove four and a half hours by air conditioned bus. We saw town after town. People look happier. I noticed different shades of people. Also I noticed that many men in some areas wore tennis shoes. We went to a doctor's house for lunch. His house was beautiful and faced the ocean. We really enjoyed the food. With such a large group, it's hard to get to know everyone's names. We will be wearing name tags. We are in Zambales. One funny thing that happened was that the bus went under some power lines. We were the first bus. The local people scattered with fear. This made all of us fearful. We joked about being electrocuted, but that is how we handled our fear. [We joked that if we made it through the second bus could go.] When we finally got to the resort, we were all hot and tired. You could see that the day had caught up with us. Dr. Mac suggested we go to the ocean; what a great idea. The water was so warm. We saw the sun set. We played in the water. Dr. Mac got her scrubs wet and laughed about a wet tee shirt contest. It was good after a long day. I like being with these people. Lori, my roommate, is great. She is kind but tired. The resort is older and the room is small. We share a shower with another room. We were going to be three in a room but Dr. Mac is by herself, not enough room for three suitcases. Well, I getting very tired. I'll write tomorrow.

January 15, 2006

I'm exhausted! What a day: we did sixteen cases. Some major: a radical mastectomy with oophorectomy, two cleft lips, a hysterectomy. We are all tired. The OR's are air conditioned but hot because we keep going in and out. Everyone is supportive. I felt weak at times but we allowed ourselves to rest. My leg still hurts. Please, God, give me strength.

Once again my diary does not tell the whole story. We were given a reception and breakfast of sandwiches along with a ceremony by the local people. We worked in a local hospital, President Ramon Magsaysay Memorial Hospital, Iba, Zambales, Philippines. We had three operating rooms with one room for emergency C-sections. In two of the operating rooms, we would have two patients at a time, and in the other, only one case. Outside each room we had a boarding schedule;

the doctors would meet their patients first. My job was to get the patient, bring them in, and set them up for the operation. We repaired cleft lips on children, which were the most challenging. Remember, I am not an OR nurse. I would set up the bovie pad(this a pad that acts as an insulator for the patient in OR), help put the monitor and blood pressure machine on the patient, do surgical prep if needed, add sutures and supplies as the surgeon needed, help lift the patient to the stretcher after the operation, or whatever else was needed. I was in severe pain with my knee so this was hard. I reminded the doctors that this was not what I did for a living, but I was willing to do anything. The first day is always the hardest because we don't know where things are.

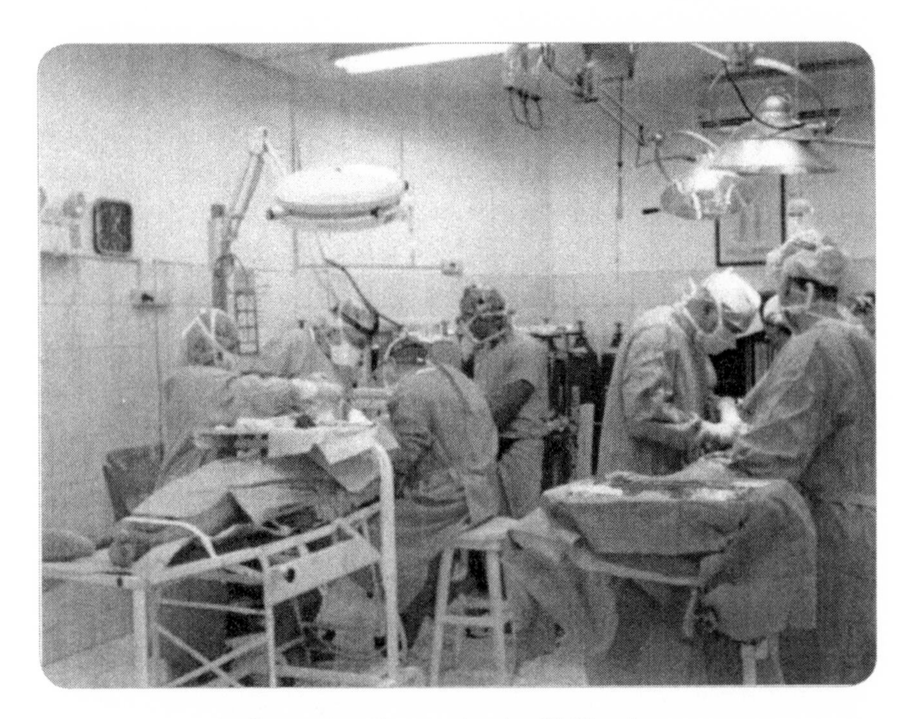

Operating Room in the Philippines

January 16, 2006

Well, another busy day. I worked the recovery room. The OR did twenty-two cases. We seem to be working better together. I was having leg pain, so I talked to two internists (MDs), who think it's ligament pain. They want me to rest so I told people of my pain and went to the recovery room. Everyone is loving, and doesn't push each other. Carla (my friend from Beaumont) is sick. I can see it in her face, so she left and went to rest. Today our patients were inguinal hernia and thyroids. I saw a doctor performing surgery in the recovery room. A worker from England brought her here. [This lady was an Aeta, a group of people who live in the mountains, tend to isolate themselves, have lots of superstitious beliefs, and believe in voodoo. So because of her beliefs, we did minor surgery in the recovery room, not in the OR.] *One of the things I didn't write about was the scooters (motorcycles): what a smell and exhaust, no emissions testing. The smell almost makes you sick. Our patients are watching me. They are all friendly and smile and call me "Madam." The weather is hot. OR and RR are air conditioned so it's a relief. The surgical ward was unbelievable. People all over the place. I don't know how the nurses keep it straight. They are so busy. They must have thirty patients to one nurse; boy, are we spoiled in the United States. The staff is working long hours. One of the techs worked four days straight without going home. His work partner was sick. Patients are moved to stretchers by strong men, no room between tables for stretchers. This means more pain for patients. No side rails on anything. It's a wonder no one is dropped. No paperwork for me in the OR, but we do have it in the RR. The medical team saw 150 patients by lunch. Dr. Mac had to leave, as her mother is dying. I'll miss her humor.*

January 17, 2006

I awoke at 0400 today; that's better than 0100 or 0200. I'm feeling better this morning. I must be getting used to the time change. After last night, my leg feels better. Every place I go, I see pictures of Christ and Mary. Outside our door is a picture of Christ. Lori and I are getting along. She is a great lady, who has a heart for the Lord. She has a beautiful spirit.

January 17,2006 1900

Day 3. Just as busy and sometimes just as stressful. After some stress in the OR, I asked Mary, our surgeon, to sing in the OR today. She has a beautiful voice and is compassionate, but she can be very difficult to work with. Dr. Smith is very fussy and wants everything just so. Carla's husband Paul, a CRNA, is great, so patient. The wards are packed with patients. People come from miles for care. We had to turn down someone who came a long way by boat. The surgical ward is overflowing, with lots of confusion. But the patients like us; they smile and are grateful. The local staff is working so hard, never losing their patience. I know they are tired and will be grateful when we are gone, like everything is back to normal. We had dinner at the beach, like a luau. We ate sitting on the sand on banana leaves. Good food: fish, watermelon, pork, chicken. We had music and torches and a bonfire. I took my shoes off and put my feet in the ocean. Paul walked with me. The stars were so bright. I just noticed that the resort has an armed guard. Also for dinner there were six guards, some things don't change.

The luau was something I will always remember. It was a beautiful night, we were sitting by the China Sea. I was told if I swam across I would hit Vietnam. The food was good. I do have a funny story about this. One of the doctors didn't know this, but we would put the bones from the food on the sand. He didn't know this, so he put his bones back on the table, and because it was dark, the person next to him couldn't see that there was no food on the bones, so he would pick up the discarded food and wonder why there was no meat on the bones. We laughed so hard when we heard this. One thing I remember about that night was looking at the stars in the sky. It was so dark, and the stars were so bright. I just wanted to stay there forever. I was the last one to leave the beach that night.

January 19, 2006

We are finished! We finished at 1500. It's hot and the sun is still out. I'm going to the beach and will write later. Back from the beach. The water is so warm. The vendors were all over us. I bought some bracelets for the kids. I saw local people fishing in the ocean; they were pulling large nets. The doctors and Patty joined in. They were so excited to be fishing. A local man came with a boat to take them snorkeling. We watched the sun set, very beautiful. We talked to some local people. I am always aware of what I show of America. Most of the people have smiles on their faces. I really love being with our group. Dr. Smith is very hard to work with. He wants everything just so, but he is a good surgeon. Good thing I have been a nurse for a long time. I don't take it personally. Edward is thirty-one years old and studying to be a doctor in the Philippines but working in the United States at Oakwood. He will make a great doctor; he was a gift.

*Mary, the surgeon, was unable to walk well this morning to get on the bus. She said it was the Ambien she took last night. I'm not so sure. I took her in a room to lie down; no one would let her operate till she slept. We moved our cases around till she was in a better state. The people of the Philippines were smiling as we left. We repaired ten cleft lips, hernia, TAH,(Total Abdominal Hysterectomy) thyroids. God, thank you for allowing me to come. I will do this as long as I can. Most of the people here are older than me. We went to the luau. We had awards with the local people, the hospital staff was there. We were all given awards. A prayer was said, and Mary sang; she has a beautiful operatic voice. The song brought tears to my eyes. I went up and thanked her for singing in OR. [*The song she sang that night was the one she sang in OR, she was practicing for that evening.*] We saw native dancers on beach. Then we ate roast pig; the food was so good. We also danced the night away. I shouldn't have danced, but I was with my friends, having fun. Lana and Dr. Ron did ballroom dancing. They were so good. I really enjoyed myself, went to bed, tired.*

The thing I felt watching the fishermen that day was what it was like in Christ's time when the fishermen threw out their nets. The nets were old, and it looked like the whole village was working together for the catch of the day. Sitting there on the beach, I could see Jesus calling the apostles to throw down their nets and follow him. Why does it take me going so far away from home to see Jesus? I felt so peaceful sitting there. I saw the Bible coming alive.

The boat that came to take my friends snorkeling was old, and that's why I didn't go with them. I remember doing the surgical scrub on a patient who was having a mastectomy; as I did this prep, I felt the hardest non-lactating breast I have ever felt. I am a breast-feeding consultant, so I have felt women's breast. I was shocked at what I felt; her breast had knots, lumps, and dark areas. I wanted to cry, as she was only thirty-four years old, and we all knew this was cancer. This was the patient we did an oophorectomy on, so that she might have a few more months of life. I also knew she would have probably no follow-up chemo or radiation. Again, I was glad for our medical care.

Being in the OR and seeing the cleft lips and palate repairs was the most rewarding. These children were older than they would have been in the United States. This means that they would probably had more stares and had been made fun of by other children. Dr. Smith was the surgeon doing the repairs. He is a gifted plastic surgeon. His wife, Kathy, was the scrub nurse for him. The scrub nurse hands the instruments to the surgeon and remains sterile. Just like the surgeon, they do not leave the patient's bedside. Dr. Smith challenged both me and Kathy; she normally worked as a floor nurse, not in the OR. He would become quite upset with both of us. He had left special gloves for himself but never told me that they were only for him, and then he became quite angry with me when I gave them to another doctor. Kathy apologized for him to me; I told her I could see he was gifted and I was not offended. All of this just made me glad that I don't work OR.

One of my happiest memories is of looking at the smile on the face of a mother whose child we had repaired the cleft lip on. She had joy on her face. I can only imagine what it was like to see her child live with this every day. I wondered if this child had trouble eating or talking. This is the hard part of not knowing the patients and no follow-up.

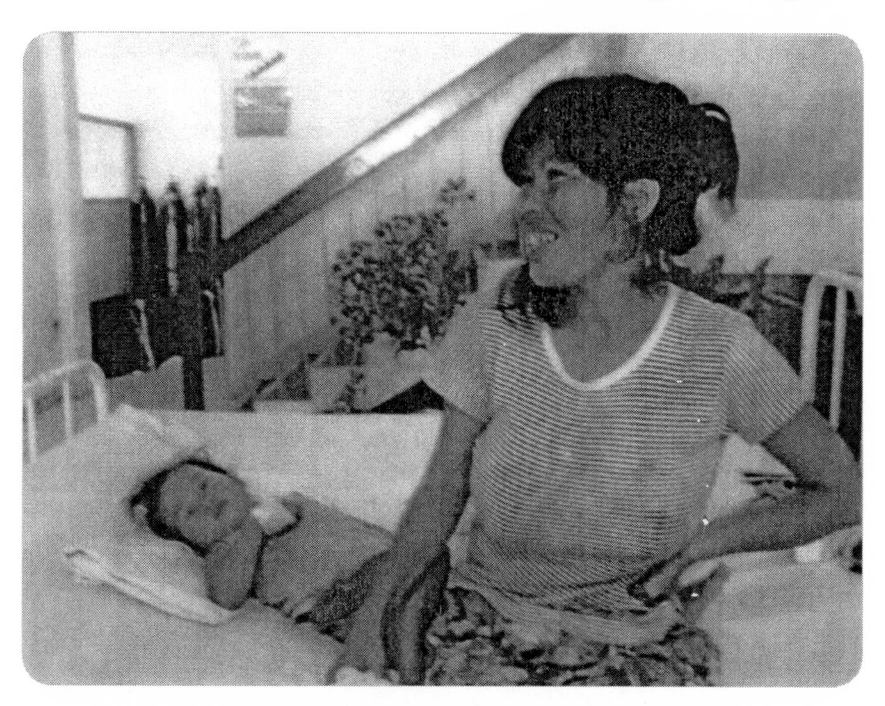

Smiling Mom after child's lip repair

January 20, 2006

We are leaving; half of the group is gone. It's already hot, and I wish I could go to the beach. It will be sad to leave. So much has happened to me. One speaker last night said you would love this work and be back, or hate it and go only go once. How can I explain to people what it's like to help people, people who really need it? How can I tell them how people live? God, whatever I'm to do with this experience, I will do. Thank you for allowing me to use my skills. I forgot to talk about the people who peddle jewelry. It's so hard not to buy. For me, not knowing the money, I'm not sure. I did buy some jewelry for Alyssa, Brittany(Rich's daughter), and Amanda(our neighbor). They bartered for the price. One woman got angry with the others about us buying from them.

Both trips in the bus took us through Subic Bay, the American naval base. I was quite impressed with what I saw. We rode up a hill so we looked into the bay. The Navy is no longer there but you could just imagine this being a busy place. Now it looked like a ghost town; all the business had left. When we went through, it was like being in an American town, modern. The buildings reminded me of home. But before and after the town, you could see poverty. I really can't imagine why they didn't want the naval base there, for commerce if nothing else.

January 21, 2006

I was able to call Rick last night to let him know I was okay. We went to a mall. It was bigger than Great Lake Crossing, three floors. I looked at the Versace store. I bought two books on the Philippines and also a journal. We went to a Mass in the middle of the mall. We were late but received Communion. The mass was packed. They had four Masses every day, with seven on Sunday. The songs were beautiful. It was hard to walk with Lori. The mall was so crowded and she didn't know where she wanted to go. We went to Bubba Gump's for dinner. I was happy. Lori would like to go somewhere else. I felt like I was back home. I wish I was flying home tomorrow. It's hard being in a strange land. I miss my family and husband. I don't know what I'm to learn. I'm at the hotel till 2130, till Lavinia picked me up. I have diarrhea now. Hope that goes away soon. I went out to lunch with Carla, she is so sweet. We know each other from Beaumont and because of her daughter and my son. She went through some things with her daughter. There are no accidents, God does put people together. I'm sitting at the pool, writing. It's cloudy but hot. I'm not swimming just enjoying. It noisy here at times; like in other places in the world, they honk to pass.

I'm amazed at myself that I didn't write about a trip we took. The doctor in charge of the group arranged for us to go on a tour of Malacanang Palace. This is like the White House. I really enjoyed this trip. Lori was not sure if she wanted to go or leave to be with her family. She chose to come with us, and she had so much fun. We traveled by bus to the palace and had a private tour with a young man as a guide. The palace was in the middle of town with guards, but unlike the White House, there were buildings close to it. I'm not Filipino but I found being there so interesting. I saw these beautiful shell windows. I had never seen shell windows, and I love shells so I thought these windows were so beautiful. We saw pictures of the presidents of the Philippines (past and current). Lori had to have her picture with one of them; she said she looked like her. We sat at a big table at which important decisions were made. We went by where General Dwight D. Eisenhower's office was when he was stationed in the Philippines. We saw the balcony where the Marcos's stood before they left the Philippines. We saw the painting that was given by the pope to the people of the Philippines. We saw the full-length paintings of the Marcos's. We did not see all of Imelda's shoes, but we saw a display of her shoes and Ferdinand's hats.

There were only about twenty of us in the group, so this was a treat, as there were no other tours. What impressed me was that I could touch things; we saw a photo album of the Marcos's trip to Indonesia, and we picked up the book and looked at photos of that trip. What a gift. I learned about history. I could see the love the people of the Philippines had for their country. We stood by a map and all of my friends showed me where they were from.

After our tour, we went back to the hotel, and Lori left me to visit her family. She had told me she would have taken me to meet her family, but all they would do was sit around and talk in their native language and I would be bored, so it was arranged that I would go with Lavinia, who I met at church. Lori forgot to tell her family I wasn't coming, and I found out later that they had roasted a pig because I was coming. I have always felt the love and care of my Filipino friends. I was touched by this, even though I never ate the pig.

January 22, 2006

I lost a day of not writing. I sat by the pool and went up to Carla and Paul's room (they went to visit family, so I was alone) and watched TV and worked on Bible study. I hate being alone. I was very tired and sleepy. I called for a wake-up call in forty-five minutes but ended up working on my Bible study; my stomach was better but still cramping. Lavinia will be picking me up. She was tired from her work in the Philippines but warm and friendly. We went to her cousin Barbara and Walt's house; it was very nice. This was their home while in the Philippines; they lived in Arizona.

Walt was a doctor and Barbara a medical technician. They have a small TV, chairs, kitchen, dining room table, two bedrooms, and a bath upstairs. I have one bedroom and Lavinia has the other. The houses were close together but not attached. There is a vacant lot next door. Barbara and Walt have a driver, Cliff. All the houses are gated. There is a guard to get into their subdivision. They have a piano, garden, and open air laundry with a small washing machine. They have a maid, Pandsy, who doesn't seem to understand me well. Pandsy has three children and seven grandchildren. She makes meals and attends to our needs.

We went with Lavinia's cousins to a beautiful church in Manila. They said the church was only two years old but looked much older. We met the priest and he blessed something Lavinia had brought. We missed Mass. We went to the water in what they call the reclaimed area. They built a strong wall to keep the water out and now have a new area for growth. There is a big shopping mall going there; Sonia and Lavinia tell me that this will be the largest mall in Asia. We ate lunch. I'm eating soup and rice.

We went to Sonia's house. There was a fight on TV: a Filipino boxer, Paket, and a Mexican boxer, Morales. Everyone is watching. Sonia's house is two stories with nice decorations drawn by Sonia's son. He is good and I encouraged him to call Disney for a job. They offer me ice cream; I pass on the ice cream because of my stomach. I never pass on ice cream.

The Filipino boxer wins. They are happy. I had to laugh because we go to the ECOPARK without traffic, and when we came back, there was lots of traffic. It seems everyone was watching the fight. We visit the ECOPARK in the middle of town (Quezon City), this ecological park. We went for a walk, it's nice, lots of nature, a swimming pool with salt water and solar heat. We don't get to see the pool up close, and there is a charge. The park has benches for picnics, a bike trail, walking trails, camping, and beautiful flowers. Sonia asked if we want to shop. Lavinia and I are tired, so we just want to rest. Sonia and her husband work for the government and drive one hour each way to work. They can get government housing that they can own. Once again I find the people to be warm. We went back to Barbara's and watch TV. I don't like the TV here very much. I can't understand some of the stations. I see a commercial for skin whitener. When are we as a race going to get it right? White people tan, dark people lighten; pretty silly.

January 23, 2006

We will be going shopping today. Hope I find some good bargains. Later that day: I bought myself some pearls. For $120, I bought Gina a necklace and earrings. The shopping mall is crowded and Lavinia did all the talking. I bought shirts for the girls and a shirt for Rick; I hope he likes it. We went to a shrine this morning. People follow me everywhere we go. They know I'm American and think that means money. I guess it means more money than they have. I'm reminded of Christ's word that the poor will be with us always. I wonder if the saints struggled with these issues. When I went to the shrine, I reminded myself that I will do God's will. I'm scared to go to Bangladesh. I'm feeling better but don't want to be sick. I think of Mother Theresa of India. Did she struggle the same way I am? I struggle to let God take control of my life. Fear is something I must work against. I will be surrounded by people who love God. I will keep asking for strength and wisdom. The Serenity Prayer will help me.

January 24, 2006

Happy birthday to me! Well, I will celebrate in two countries if you call waking up at 0230 in the Philippines celebrating. It was early in the morning when we went to the airport. Much less traffic but there still was some parts of the city awake; the market was still awake. It's a city that doesn't sleep. Lavinia went with us. I thanked Cliff and gave him some money. I thanked Barbara and Walt last night. They will be in my heart always. I wish I would have bought two travel books (1,000 Places to See before You Die, Traveler's Journal) so I could have given Barbara one. We went to a prayer service last night for a cousin of Lavinia. It's the custom of people in the Philippines to have a prayer service for nine days after someone dies, then a year of mourning. We had a big meal; I met cousins and I also met a doctor from the Philippines. He had trained in the States and said he had been to Detroit once. Once again everyone is warm and friendly, and I enjoy being with them. I will never forget my trip but I'm happy to be going home. The trip is only eleven hours, shorter than the trip to the Philippines. The pilot said we would be arriving twenty minutes early. I still can't believe all the experiences of the trip.

I would celebrate my birthday in three countries: Philippines, Japan (because we had a layover there), and the United States. I still think of that birthday as pretty neat, and I love thinking about my birthday in three countries.

February 11, 2006

It's been a month since I returned from the Philippines. It's been a very stressful month. I would be excited about Bangladesh and then worried. I would try to live in the moment. Every time I was with Dr. Lee and the group, I was fine. I was going to be Soo's roommate and was quite excited about that. When I was away, I would be worried and scared but kept telling myself to live in the moment. I made plans but did not plan the outcome. My visa came in four days. I got the time off of work, and two weeks before, Dr. Geimer said go with her blessing. I felt God has given me directions. I was always nervous. I wondered if I could do it. Dr. Lee felt that I should go. I felt a lot of pressure to make the second trip. I was trying to do God's will. I wanted to go in my mind but my body wasn't doing well. My blood pressure was up, off and on.

February 21, 2006

I never finished that day. On the Wednesday before I was to go, February 8, my blood pressure was up, and I was not feeling well. I took my Toprolol early and went to dinner with Sharon. My knee hurt. Sharon and I went to LaShieh. I then went to the church for our meeting. I was happy to be with Dr. Lee and the group; we were happy to go to Bangladesh. I went to my meeting, spoke of my fears, and thought I was doing well. Took Mefloquine (malaria medicine) on the way home. I felt funny and took my blood pressure when I came home: 180/99. I took a sleeping pill and went to bed.

I woke from a dead sleep at 0230 with my heart racing, head pounding, feeling like I had a drug reaction. Call Dr. Geimer, blood pressure still up, she didn't answer; woke Rick up and asked to go to Emergency; during the drive, I felt sick. When I arrived in ER, my blood pressure was 202/108. I saw the doctor, rested, had lab and EKG, and was sent home after two hours; blood pressure 150/90. The ER doctor said I should seriously consider not going on the trip. I took the day off and rested all day; blood pressure: 140/80. I went to work Friday, blood pressure: 160/90. I talked with Dr. Geimer (not able to see her because of work), and she told me I could not go. I was too unstable with my blood pressure and my knee. My x-ray showed some damage to my knee. I cried!

At work, I went to talk to a coworker, who took my blood pressure: 188/98. I took my prescription as ordered. Went home; my blood pressure was up all night. I took my prescription, up to 200 mg, the highest allowed; my blood pressure was finally down. Saturday, after much thought, I called and talked to Soo Lee and told her my doctor's advice. She was so sweet; we both cried. Soo told me I needed to rest, and we had lots of places to go together. My blood pressure was stable all day. I told Sharon and Rick what was going on. I went to church Sunday; I talked to Toots and went to the prayer service. Soo wanted me to go in front of the church. I did. Toots, Connie, and Soo told me to come, and they would take care of me. Dr. Lee said I looked flushed. I was feeling fine till I thought about going against medical advice.

The rest of the day was hard. I knew my blood pressure was up, and I kept taking extra Toprolol, up to 175 mg, but refused to take my blood pressure till I felt better; it was 160/98. I packed to go. We had our meeting, and I let everyone say good-bye to me like I was going, but I still wasn't sure. I would live in the moment. I couldn't sleep all night. I tossed and turned. I took a sleeping pill, drank Sleepy Time tea, took a bath, had sex, Rick gave me a back rub, watched TV—everything I knew to help but couldn't sleep. I was too unstable; my blood pressure in the morning was 218/108.

I called Dr. Lee and told him I couldn't go. I was too unstable; my blood pressure went down, so I decided to see my friends off. I couldn't have them leave without praying for them. Dr. Lee was so gracious and prayed for me, saying that part of the team was missing. I cried. They were making the trip, and he was praying for me.

It's has been a week since they have gone. I'm feeling better, blood pressure is 130/88. I'm still taking higher medicine. My knee still hurts. I had a stress test and x-ray. All my friends were relieved that I didn't go. They all thought I didn't look well enough to make the trip. All except Rick; he would have liked me to go. I have been thinking about my friends all the time, I pray for their safe return. I wonder where they are and hope they're safe. I also wish I could be with them. I still feel like I let fear get the best of me. I want to be super human. I wonder how Mother Theresa did the things she did. I keep wondering if I'll go again. I want to go. I don't want my fears to keep me from doing things. People tell me maybe I should do things here in the United States. I don't think they understand how the rest of the world lives. I guess I didn't understand also. I believe God helped me become a nurse for some reason. I want to give back. I feel God has put a burning desire in my heart. I feel that I have let God down. I can't help thinking if I had more faith, I could have gone.

I am making the most of my time, making curtains and redoing the house. I really don't understand why I couldn't go, but I'm trying to accept God's will in my life.

One of the things I learned about life as a result of not being able to make this trip was to make plans and not to plan the outcome. God is in charge. I found myself confronting my shame once again, the shame of not being good enough. I could not call my friends from work and tell them, because what would they think? I didn't even tell my in-laws that I didn't go for about a week. I knew that God had told me I would go back to Bangladesh, so why didn't I go?

Still to this day, I feel like I stepped out of God's plan on that trip. I had asked Dr. Mac to take me to the Philippines, but Dr. Lee was taking too long to ask me again, and I wanted to go somewhere. I went after Dr. Mac and kept after her to take me. When Dr. Lee asked me,

I had plane tickets to the Philippines already but couldn't say no to Dr. Lee. Once again I had to look deep inside myself at my motives and how I needed to be more in touch with God's will in my life. I was told that they really could have used me in Bangladesh and they were short a recovery room nurse. One of the interesting facts about that trip was that the CRNA who went on that trip was later fired from her job and committed suicide. One of the interesting things I learned when I went to the Philippines was how to work in the OR, and this will be helpful in a third world country in a hospital setting. I saw so many more operations than we were able to do in Bangladesh. I feel that I will be better able to be useful because of this experience.

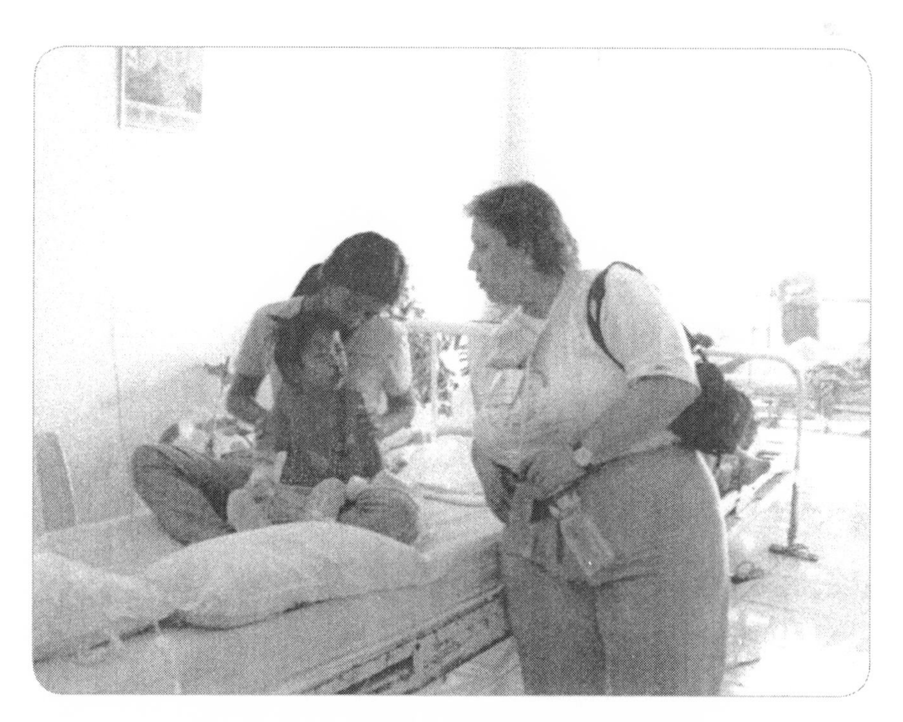

Vicki and a patient after cleft lip repair

CHAPTER 6:

Back to the Philippines.

January 18, 2007

I'm on the plane again; this time, I'm going back to the Philippines. It was a good thing I didn't go to Bangladesh. One day, I finally looked at my prescription for Benicar. I had the doctor's office call in a prescription for this medication, and they did not add HCT (a diuretic). When I was at home, Dr. Geimer would write me prescriptions with HCT, but when I went on my trips, I took it without HCT. I would have been in real trouble.

Dr. Lee was great and asked me to go again. We didn't go in 2006, and he is not planning to go till November 2007. So I asked my friends if I could go to the Philippines, and they said yes, so I'm on my way. I will room with Patty. Mike is back, and Paul is back. Two CRNA students, Tara and Judy, are also with us. Dr. Mac is already there. She called me and may have a first class seat for me on the way back; I'm on stand-by for now. The flight is packed again. Dr Mac and I had a long talk last week. I will carry her bag again, heavier than mine. Most people at work have been supportive, and as always, Rick has been supportive. I feel more calm this time. I'm feeling better, no hurting knee. I thought maybe God didn't want me to do this anymore, but everything fell into place.

My friend Joyce lost her daughter. The funeral is tomorrow. I feel bad that I won't be there, but we did talk and she understands. I'm so glad to have good friends. I plan on bringing jewelry back for my friends.

January 19, 2007

Well, we arrived safely. By the time we got to our hotel, it was 0300 (Philippines time), a long day. Both Patty and I fell right asleep. We were back up by 0630. I did sleep well. It was good to be flat. Our room is better than last year, shower similar to Bangladesh, no curtain; we also sometimes have to flush with the bucket. This is a resort with a swimming pool. We went to Intramurals and Fort Santiago. I learned a lot about the Philippines and its history. Our guide was from California. Our Philippines friends said he knew more about Philippines history than they did. We visited Manila Hotel, where General Macarthur stayed during the war. The Philippines was originally a Spanish colony and has played an important role in history, including religious history. We ate at a restaurant, good food. The Filipinos like sharing their food with us. We rode on a horse-drawn carriage. Mike the CRNA is back. While at Intramurals we saw these children on small boats (very dangerous); they were begging for money. Paul didn't have change and I gave them coins. Paul said that made him happy. I didn't want to fall off the ledge so I didn't see. I'm getting sleepy so I will write tomorrow.

Intramural and Fort Santiago were beautiful. Intramural is an old group of buildings which includes a church. We went for a ride in a horse-drawn cart, the cart was dressed in traditional Spanish costume. At the top of the fort, boys were down in a boat trying to get money. I wouldn't have thrown money except Paul encouraged me.

January 20, 3007

I slept good last night except for being up three times to the bathroom. I changed my blood pressure medication with HCT to evenings, so I'm up. I will get that back on the right times, sometime. I'm sitting on our balcony watching hundreds of little birds in the tree. They are chirping and moving from branch to branch. I want to see the sun rise over the mountains off our balcony. We are on the third floor (no elevators). Everything is so green here; it also cold at night (comfortable, not cold). We are in the cooler season. Everyone tell us summer is hot here. Last night we saw the darkest sky with many stars, just like I saw on the beach last year. My roommate (Patty) and I are getting along well. She is great and hard working. She is the only scrub nurse in the group. The group has to hire more. I with I could but I never have and now is not the time to teach me.

Mike is up enjoying, the view like me. He was born in the Philippines but left when he was five, so being here is good for him. He will meet his parents here. He is such a nice young man. We did karaoke last night; that was fun. We had a roast pig, the fruit here is so good, and things you wouldn't see in the States. The mangos are wonderful. I have been told this is the off season for fruits. If this is off season, I can't imagine what it tastes like in season. Once again I wonder why I'm here, but God knows the reason. I will follow him; I want to do his will. The poverty here reminds me how blessed I have been. For some people, it's been a very hard life. The Philippines have 7,000 islands that go from north to south; with all the green, that must be so beautiful. Life in Manila must be hard, like any big city; lots of traffic, many cars, busses, and motorcycles. The pollution is hard. You see many people covering their faces as they wait for busses. We always have air conditioning on so we don't get the fumes. We see several people wave at us. I love it when the children wave. But we even had young men wave; I think they see Judy and Tara, that's why they wave.

January 22, 2007

I didn't get to write yesterday. We spent the morning swimming; the sun felt good and warm during the day. Then we attended a Mass just for the group. That was nice. The priest was from Nevada. He had a good sermon. The one reading was about how we are one body and many parts. I thought about how in our group, we are different with different skills, all from different backgrounds and different cultures. We went to the hospital to unpack, lots of confusion. We have three ORs this year but only two are connected. We really need scrub nurses. The rooms and the hospital are smaller than last year, some good equipment, and some poor equipment. We finished about 1700. A few of us—Mike, Paul, Tara, Judy, Patty, and Laura—went to the market. Patty felt unsafe. Judy and Tara were excited. I don't think they realized just how people look at us. Patty was very aware of the stares. I had already experience that in Bangladesh, so I was not surprised. The market was full of many things to buy, a bakery, fruit market, fish market, shoes, etc. We spent a long time there and missed the bus. We had a car take us home. Then the congressman who built the hospital gave us a banquet. They had dancers dressed in native costumes doing native dances. The costumes were bright. The banquet lasted till 2200. Once again we were so tired.

Well, let me catch up with today. We were one hour late getting to the hospital. The bus was late, so we started behind. Then we had no water (the congressman's wife thinks it was sabotaged). Then we had no cautery. We burned out the OR light in the middle of an operation. They ran two operations in my room at a time. It's hard when both tables want instruments or other things at the same time. Once again I'm challenged. We had a thyroid case with three lobes; it went all the way to the ear. I'm so glad I live where I could get treatment. I feel bad not knowing the instruments. I feel helpless.

January 23, 2007

Well, another day of busy surgery. We are doing better. I'm feeling better about how things are going. It's still hard doing two cases at a time. What seems to happen was the cases start at the same time and finish at the same time, too many people in the room, all wanting to be sterile at the same time. Dave is a local nurse. He knows a lot and is very nice, but OR is not his job. He is getting tired from all the work. The congressman and his wife are sweet. They are feeding us and working hard to make us feel good. I finally saw Dr. Mac today. She is staying in our hotel. She sat on the bus with me. She is so sweet. I see Lavinia here and there. She will be staying with me in Manila. I'm glad because I like being with her. Dr. Black is funny. Most of the other doctors are very patient with us. Some people do more sitting than others. Laura and her sister Baba are sweet. I stood on the balcony this morning, talking to her. She is a widow with three children; she lives here. I am so grateful I live in the United States after seeing the thyroids. I talked to Rick today. He sounded different. He said that Mark got a full time job with benefits. Hurray! I wish I could say I miss home but I'm too busy.

We stayed in two different hotels because of the number of the group, the surgical group in one hotel and the medical team in another hotel. This is why I didn't always see Lavinia. We did eat in the hotel I stay in.

January 24, 2007

Happy birthday to me! Happy birthday to me! Well, I'm fifty-six and I feel like a hundred. Another busy day, we did lots of cases. We are working together better. We understand each other better. We did a case on a child to repair his colostomy, which he had had since infancy. It was a fascinating case; we took lots of bowel out, but when the surgeon was checking the bowel, he found a hard stool and a long worm, between ten and twenty inches long and moving. The surgeon was quite happy he checked, he did a good job with the surgery, and I told him so. After we left, the child took a turn for the worse, needed blood, needed intubation, and was not doing well. I don't know what happened yet, the crew wasn't back yet. I wanted to stay there but there were enough people, and I would just be in the way. It is so hard seeing what a difference in medical care poor countries have compared to ours. We did a hernia (bilateral) on a young man; he walked two days to have surgery.

January 25, 2007

Well, the work is over.

We had three Vickis in the OR at one time: Vicki, Vicki, and Vicki. All three of us were Victoria but wanted to be called Vicki. You can imagine the confusion when someone called Vicki; we also had fun with it. One of the things that happened in the OR that was interesting was, because we used spinal tray meds that were expired, a tall Filipino man was moving his legs during a hernia surgery. He was trying to get up in the middle of surgery. The CRNA immediately gave him IV sedation.

I find it interesting now that I never wrote what happened to the little boy. I think that for many reasons I blocked out the fact that he died . Not only he died, but as I write this, I noticed that he died on my birthday. I think all of us involved in his case doubted ourselves, and I know I doubted myself. The hard part about doing this kind of work is we don't know the history of the patients; I don't even know their names or their ages. I know that the grandparents brought this little boy for surgery. We didn't know how long he had the colostomy or why. We thought that maybe he had worms since birth. Some of my doctor friends said that worms can go to the heart or lungs. Was this the only worm? The pediatricians would have cleared him for OR but they saw him only once. His death was the first and only death this organization ever had. All of us in the OR that day will remember this case. The CRNA could not come back to work the next day. Those of us who work in medicine do so because we love patients and love the work, so when something doesn't go well or the outcome is not positive, we feel it. What happened? What did we do? What did we miss? Did this patient have the right IV solution? Did he suffer septic shock because someone broke sterile technique, were the right solutions used for irrigation, was the patient intubated or sedated too long, especially after we found the worm? Not one of us knows the plans God has for us, even in death. Also Satan would have us stop, get discouraged, and never use our gifts again for good. I don't know if I would have remembered this child if the outcome was not death, but I do remember him, and to me, he is like the thousands of children in the world who live in poverty.

January 26, 2007

I was too tired to write last night. We didn't get back till 2000, and then we went to a party with the congressman. They gave us a plaque. The surgeon sang again. We were all upbeat. We, all of us (dentist, medical, pediatrics, minor and major surgery), saw 3,630 patients. We were so busy on the last day. I was in the room with two OR tables. We could only do spinal on one table and the other was for major operations. Most of the spinals were waking up and moving their feet. We would have thirteen to fifteen people in the room at one time. I would have to get on the ground and change the bovie pad cord because we had only one machine between two cases. I'm not familiar with surgical instruments, so it was quite a challenge. Sometimes people would be asking for things at the same time. It's hard to decide what to do first. Thank God for Dave. He worked so hard. The last day he was scrubbed till 1500 with no lunch, sweating and standing. I told him that he had to get lunch and drink a whole bottle of water before he came back. He started calling me "Mom"; I told him I could be his mother. It was hard to leave him. Dave was so great. He was so sweet.

January 28, 2007

I was too tired to finish writing. On the 27th, we arrived at the Holiday Inn Manila around 1200 after waiting for Judy and Tara. They were out swimming till 0400 and then no one woke them up, so much for the 0700 leave time. The traffic going to Manila was long. It's so hard to see the poverty and the crowded population. We went to Greenhill and bought Geri (a coworker from the hospital) pearls. I lost my money, over $200. I tried to take this in good spirit. I had to go to the bathroom and was in a hurry; it cost 10 pesos and I rushed to get my money and must have dropped it on the ground. Everyone was kind to me and worried about me and wanted the best for me.

Lavinia took us to Greenhill's again. Patty loved the way Lavinia would barter. She would get her some good prices. After I lost my money, I didn't feel like I could buy much there. I did some calculating, and Patty and Lavinia paid me for the room, and I now have extra money. We went to an Asian market in their Chinatown and I bought some things. Then Dr. Mac's sister-in-law and J.P. took us to the Mall of Asia. I bought the most beautiful pictures, coffee, and snacks. We spent the rest of the evening just quiet and slept four hours. I am very sleepy now. I was able to swim yesterday. I felt so good. It was nice to see the sun and feel the warmth.

It's funny, even on the fifth floor you hear the traffic, police blowing their whistles and the noise of the traffic. I'm finding it hard to leave. I just started to think about all the things I have to do at home. It's like I have been away forever. I miss home but I have been so busy. I am aching and started my period two days ago, and of course I didn't bring enough supplies, and they don't sell tampons except OBs. I can't believe I'm still having a period. Thank God it wasn't while the medical work was going on. I bleed through my clothes twice. This is getting hard! People keep telling me of the benefits but it's hard for me to believe. My feet are pretty swollen. I keep taking my pills and now I added Cipro. It can be confusing when I should take them.

Guess what? I'm riding first class. Dr. Mac gave me a certificate for first class. I love this and have good seats for both flights. I'm on the second level this time. I can't believe how nice this is. Thank you, God, for this gift!

The reason I lost the money was because I was trying to go to the bathroom and was bleeding very hard. At that mall, you had to pay to go to the bathroom, and I could not get the money out quick enough. I must have dropped the money on the ground in a hurry. I did bleed through my clothes. Losing money is never easy, but after all the years of talking about accepting things you can't change, I was able to let go of the money and still enjoy the rest of the shopping trip. The Mall of Asia was a wonderful experience with some great food. I had coconut juice in a coconut.

Getting to ride first class was wonderful, as I slept and was able to stay up when I got home for several hours. My experiences in the Philippines will always be with me. The spirit of the people will always be with me. I can tell you I know what Balut is. I have had holo-holo(a Filipino desert) and loved it. I have seen the hospitals that people can go to, and I know the difference we have here. I have been in shopping malls where there are armed guards and all the Filipinos had their bags checked but I did not. I saw a poster for breast-feeding that had a white child pictured and I felt that was odd; why not a Filipino child? Then I realized how much we influence the rest of the world; they want to be like us.

CHAPTER 7:

Really, Dr. Lee, a second time?

January 17, 2008

Well, I am sitting in the Northwest lounge, waiting for my flight to Bangladesh. I made it! I feel good! Of course, I felt sick last week. I had to go on antibiotics. Dr. Geimer was so supportive. Rick has always been supportive. My friends have been supportive, Prudi Manzella, collected money. I really did not know what to do with that. I wasn't sure if I should keep it. I was going to donate it to Chilmary Medical Center, but they only collected $55. I was confused that the amount was $55; maybe that way, I knew I was just meant to give the money away. I wish my friends would understand. I'm not sure why God has taken me on this wonderful journey. I saw Judy from last year at the airport; they were on their way to the Philippines. I wish I was going there but God had something else in mind. I'm with great people who I love. Toots, Connie, Dr. Lee, and Soo have become great friends. I will be roommates with Eun Jin Lee. What a difference; I can say her name. She is young and exciting, and I like her already. Things that have happened in my life: I now have a grandson, Gina's baby, Gibson Paul, is nine months old and crawling.

January 19, 2008

Bancock, Thailand

We are on the plane to Bangladesh, finally. We arrived in Thailand late, and we had some confusion. We meet Heidi and Miekie. Heidi has done medical work in different countries before. She lives in Idaho, and Miekie lives in Portland, Oregon. Miekie is African American. What a group we are, so multicultural. This is a good thing. We will be able to show how different people can live together. We were able to sleep for a few hours. It felt so good. I slept well. The airport in Thailand looked so different. Thailand looked so much cleaner. We had to wait in the airport again, as the flight was delayed.

Hotel in Bangladesh

We are halfway there; what a day, two and a half hours on the plane. Six to seven hours on the bus. We had two busses. Connie, Toots, Eun Jin, Hong, and Dr. Pak are on the bus with us. The driver was Walter; he was patient with us. He could speak a little English. Bangladesh looks different. We got through customs without problems—all of us. Director Chang was there to meet us. What a joy it was to go through so quickly. We took a ride through town. Things look better here. I didn't feel the spirit of poverty like I did the first time. I had my first experience of going to the bathroom using a hole in the ground. I had to laugh because I ended up with my underwear almost in the hole. We arrived and had dinner. We are staying in a four star hotel with a swimming pool. The prime minister made it, along with a new hospital. Director Chang says we were the first foreign visitors because it cost too much; the beds were hard but I will enjoy it for the night.

I didn't swim in the pool. One thing they told me was that the hotel emptied and filled the pool daily; I found that odd. My friend laughed at me for even trying to go to the bathroom in the hole in the ground. The ground was wet, and I almost slipped in the hole; also, having pants on does not help. I can see why dresses are much easier. I guess I really had to go to the bathroom on that stop but I did learn a lesson on how to travel. Also I wrote we were on a bus, but really it was a van.

January 20, 2008

What a day. I tried to write in the bus but couldn't, so I gave up and was too tired to write later.

January 21, 2008

We have arrived at the compound. Yesterday was filled with more travel, another four hours by bus. My legs are so swollen. We went with Director Chang to the leprosy compound. Madame Yoo was there. It was good to see her. What a difference from a few years ago. I'm seeing first hand the power of a vision. I guess I have never been much of a visionary, due to my negative nature. The children follow us around, everywhere. They greet us with "Good morning, madam." One spoke to me in English, and I answered her back in English. They are the future of the community. At the compound we saw lots of vegetables. They are developing a new date that grows in this area, and this will open this area to trade; they are also fishing with fish and shrimp, which they don't have in this area.

The house where Madame Yoo lives has filtered water, tiled floor, electric, A.C, satellite TV, a room for guests, all the comforts of home. All in all, she remains lonely because of the cultural differences and her faith. One thing I noticed this year is that people were waving as the bus went by. That showed me that they are seeing progress. Director Chung explained that in the Muslim faith, you have a lot in life and you do not leave that. They are trying to show a different way, that you can change things. He has done so much hard work. We sort supplies after the tour. The OR is now tiled and has a door, also an OR light; it looks so much better.

I saw an old friend, Miss Chung; she looks so happy. I can see her growth. She has a young Korean nurse with her, Miss Lee. She doesn't speak English, but we are getting along. There is also a young Korean man at the compound. The OR has a second floor now. The compound is improving. We are in the master house, which looks like Madame Yoo's, tiled with an upstairs. We are all together in here.

Eun Jin had a project for school so that the students can learn English. Connie, Toots, and Miekie helped with it. We had a great time. Connie kept singing her ABCs song. She kept getting G wrong; I tried to correct her, and then I made a mistake. I enjoy being with these people. We do enjoy each other. We have prayers every morning. We sing "I Love You Lord" in English, Korean, Bengal, and Filipino (Tagalog). Toots made a great breakfast.

Afternoon

We finished the OR early. We did seven operations on women. Many had a prolapsed uterus. We are not sure why. The beginning of the day was hard, we weren't organized, but as the day went on, it was better. The women are receptive to us. I see new faces but I see some old faces. I remember the interpreter, Mrs. Cushim. She had a baby some two years ago. She is also a teacher. Miss Lee, the Korean nurse, is young and bright. We have no piggyback solution, so giving antibiotics was a challenge. It's hard but I seem to understand them better. All eyes were on us. They are very curious about us. The language is the hardest, but I smile and show kindness and use gestures. My leg hurts and I need to put my feet up from the swelling. Toots made a great meal. We enjoyed the fellowship. We are working on crafts again. Miss Lee, our nurse, took out all of our patients' IVs. We needed two left in for antibiotics. Well, I'll think of that tomorrow.

January 22, 2008

The start of another day; I woke up with a bad dream. Satan is really trying to get to me. A dream about Rick; it is hard to have that kind of dream when we are so far apart. My feet are still swollen but feel better. I woke Connie and Toots up. I tried to be quiet but the doors are so noisy that once one person is up, we are all up. I came down and found Eun Jin up working on a project, so I helped. I just remember the patient who was hugging me. These women have such a hard life. We had a twenty-five-year-old with a prolapsed uterus, so rare for someone that age. This trip is so very different. I'm not as scared. I can see God's vision for these people. I can really see God's work. I wonder why me, why here? Is it for them or is it for me? Whatever the reason, I will do your will. The verse from Matthew 5, "Blessed are the poor in spirit," came to me at prayer service; I will pray about that.

January 22,2008 1830

We did eight cases again. These women are younger than me but look so much older. They all seem to care about each other. They will look after each other. The hardest part is the language; gestures just don't make it, but with the help of the staff, it works. One patient's uterus was the size of a basketball; how painful that must have been. Miss Lee, the young Korean, is so smart; she is so happy, loving, and caring; without her I would be lost. Mrs. Cushim is the translator, and she is also the teacher. We had some down time, and we were able to talk. She is so sweet. People joined us, and the next thing we knew, the room was filled. Soo came by and really enjoyed the fact that we talked. Eun Jin had a photo day at school. The children had their best clothes on. They looked so cute. Every morning the kids do their morning routines, exercise, and pledge, and they danced for us this morning; they marched past us, saying, "Good morning, madam." You can see the joy in their spirit. You can see the joy in the eye of some of the workers.

This morning, Director Chang told us the goals for Chilmary Medical Center. They will be totally self-ruled soon. They are making a difference here. He explained that there is a large Muslim al-Qaeda cell about a hundred miles from here, so it's important for this region to have a Christian presence. My heart sank when I heard this. But I knew this when I came here. I'm with my friends and doing God's will, so whatever happens I will accept.

The conversation I had with Mrs. Cushim was an honest conversation and would lead to us becoming friends. I started talking about my life, my family, and what life was like for me in America. I told her about my father, brothers, and sisters and how we lived as children. I told her and then told those who joined us some of the details. I asked about their life and their family. I found out that Mrs. Cushim was close to her mother. We shared, laughed, and I found myself surrounded by new friends. This trip I felt I was connecting with someone. Soo came by and saw us talking. She could see that we were connecting, and she was pleased.

Morning exercises before school in Bangladesh

January 23,2008 1200

I have a few minutes to write my thoughts. I'm listening to the children singing. What hope there is in the children. I also had a child who was scared of me, crying and hiding from me. I might be the only white person they have every seen. How sad.

January 23,2008 2000

Well, we are done eating, and I'm putting my feet up. We had a busy day again. My feet are hurting again. We had a busy day, eight cases. We did one on a little eight-year-old. Her mother was crying as she went to OR. We talked through Mrs. Cushim. This woman's husband left her with two girls, eight months before. I tried to build up her self-esteem. She was beautiful; her mother was with her there. The mother said that her daughter loved her mother. It is colder than I remember last time. It rained today and rained. We had to put a plastic over our patients to carry them to the other room. It was quite a sight. Then on the way back, the workers would carry the stretchers over their heads to keep dry. We had some good laugh over this. But what I noticed is that we all worker together, even Muslims with Christians. The rain continued all night. Everything is soaked. Our trip home will be hard. We sang at night. What fun. Dr. Lee and I sorted through the supplies. We throw out a lot of things. It's really cold. I wish I would have brought warmer things.

When I read my diary, I remember so many things. The patients would be dressed in saris. I would use gestures to get them to remove their clothes. We would give each patient a scrub gown to cover themselves with; they had to be covered. Some of the women were so tiny that the gowns were way too large for then. It was very important for their heads to be covered so we would use surgical hats for them. Their hair was mostly long, some graying and unkempt. Sometimes I was afraid to touch their hair because I was afraid of lice. Aunt Anne had taught me to work past that fear. I could get treatment if needed. I forgot that it was cold, and so my patients were very cold after OR. We would cover the patients as soon as possible with the blankets they brought. Some of the blankets were old and dirty, but this was all they had. I would have the family sit by them so no one fell; you see, we had no side rails; most of them lay on tables. Because I would was the nurse in charge of pre-op and post-op, giving meds, starting IVs, and seeing patients after the operation, I would sometimes have to leave the patients. I never felt I could leave then alone even though we used spinal and IV sedation; I was always afraid that they would fall.

It was raining when we took the patients from the recovery room to the ward. They would be carried by stretcher, but because of the rain, we had to find plastic to cover them. What a sight that was! It would take more people to help with this, but we wanted to keep our patients from getting cold. One of my patients was really cold; I covered her and then noticed that the window was open and a breeze was blowing on her. I put my arm outside to close the window when I felt electricity go through my body. I had touched a wire and felt a shock like I have never felt before or since. What a scare! I told the workers, and they got right on fixing this; we did not have to go through committees or several phone calls or work orders.

I usually bring candy for the airplane ride, as I don't chew gum. I would bring my supplies with me while I took care of the patients. While we were talking, I offered candy to the workers; they would take my candy. Rupal, our boat driver, who would help me transport patients, loved the candy. He would come back looking for me to give him some candy. I would find that I was modeling behavior; when I used hand sanitizer, all the workers would use the hand sanitizer also. I would leave any personal things I had. I don't know if that was the right thing to do because I didn't have enough for everyone, but I felt close to these workers.

January 24, 2008

Happy birthday to me! Well, another year in a foreign country. What a great birthday. We did a health clinic in Ulipur, the leprosy compound. The children were so cute ("Morning, madam"); they all wave and are very curious. The doctors saw a hundred patients and we gave out medicine for a hundred people. They cooked a special meal for us, really good lamb. We were able to feed the whole compound for $150. Dr Lee did a wonderful job, talking to the group in the morning. He talked about Acts 3, where Peter and John healed the lame man, and that's what needs to happen here in Bangladesh. Dr. Lee surprised me by asking me to lead the prayer after the ground-breaking ceremony. They are adding more buildings which will house male patients. It was very humbling; I have never been asked to lead prayer in such a multicultural group.

We became friends. The local nurses have a hard exterior but do soften when we treat them well. Soo asked me to wear my Shalwar Kameez(Bangladesh dress). The locals liked that I wore it; it made me feel more like I was one of the people. I keep asking myself, Why me? What do you want me to do? I guess I should just live in the moment, and God will tell me. Director Chang told us that it will be ten hours to Dhaka by bus, so we must leave early. He also told us that there will be a meeting in Dhaka of 1.5 million Muslims. I wondered why we saw so many Imams in the airport. I guess I make good observations. My human side is scared; my faith side says we will be okay. When we came back from the island, the fountain was done and water was flowing. What a sight! There were decorations on it with sayings in English and Bengali. What craftsmen, digging this hole for a fishery. When we came back, Miss Chung, Miss Lee, and the young Korean worker made us a special dinner; it was so creative and good. What wonderful fellowship. Thank you for a great birthday! I love you, Lord!

This would be my second trip to the island, and this time we were in a motorized boat, not on the roof. This trip was different. We would see beautiful yellow flowers in bloom. We did not see any local people, and it was so peaceful. I could see the beauty of these islands.

The fountain I am talking about was made by the locals along with Mr. Kim. They worked long and hard on it. The fountain was dedicated to the people. It was exciting to see the water coming out of it. This fountain gave beauty to this place. The local people dug out the spot for the water to try to grow shrimp. Watching them would be interesting as they would dig, put dirt in buckets, and carry the dirt up a hill. All of this was done by hand, no machines.

Medical group on the islands in Bangladesh

January 25, 2008

Toots and Connie were having a conversation about age. Toots asked me directly when my birthday was, and I told her it was yesterday. Everyone wished me happy birthday and was mad that I didn't tell them. I'm learning not to be the center of attention. We ate breakfast and left on time. The trip back to Dhaka was long and tedious. We made good time; our driver was fast. We saw a huge accident on the highway. The traffic was backed up for miles, bus after bus after bus. We stopped at the same restaurant for some papaya juice. Then we kept driving and driving. The country is beautiful, lots of vegetables and fruits. We stopped for Chinese food and guess what? We saw Caucasians. When we arrived in Dhaka, I saw a real change. They have street lights and traffic lights; we saw an A&W and Kentucky Fried Chicken. We ate at a Korean restaurant. We had our final meeting with suggestions and telling what we gained. I am so grateful to be here. What a difference five years makes. There is a convention center here. There are tall buildings now where the squatters were. We went shopping and I bought a scarf. I forgot to tell you yesterday we went to the islands. They are shrinking and changing all the time.

January 26, 2008

*The Trip Home: We are on the plane for Bannock. We were up early again. Eun Jin, Connie, and Toots were talking. We had such a laugh because I was the one with a mosquito bracelet(*bracelet made with chemicals to keep mosquito away*) and guess who woke up with a bite? I heard him buzzing last night. I held my bracelet up to my face, swatted him, covered my head, and he still got me. Those bites make me nervous. We had breakfast and went on a tour of the school. We had devotions with the teachers. The school had not changed. They really need a new school. They said they are working on that. We also went to the music school. They are looking for a teacher. I could not tell Gina. I want her and Rich to be safe. We saw the office of Chilmary Medical Center. Director Chang leads such a simple life. Director Chang and Madame Chang were interviewing, so they did not come to the airport with us. Madame Yoo came with us. We will be working on a program to adopt a child; Heidi, Miekie, and Toots* *have already adopted one. I see such a change in Dhaka; it's growing. There are tall buildings going up. They have a convention center, sports center, IT center. I did not see as many squatters as I did before. Things still look dirty. I think it's all the pollution. I saw this also in the Philippines. They worry about the United States and emission controls. Bangladesh still has a problem with people throwing things on the ground. But so do we. I'm not sure what God wants me to do now. I guess I'm waiting for his direction.*

January 27, 2008

On the road again. We got up at 0300 to catch our flight. We shopped fast last night, and I bought some silk scarves. I think they will be gifts for Christmas. We went to a great Thai restaurant. We had crab (I have never had such good crab).

What a way to end this visit. I had a great time this visit, I enjoyed the company. I knew that God would take me back to Bangladesh.

CHAPTER 8:

Bangedlash again, making an impact.

December 23, 2008

The Department of State warns US citizens of the risk of travel to Bangladesh and urges caution while traveling during the period before and after the upcoming election on December 29. This travel alert expires on January 5.

Sunday before this trip, after church (St. Anastasia), Toots looked for our parish priest and had him say a blessing for a safe trip over us; he prayed over us. Toots insisted we find him for a blessing. I would not know till later just what that blessing would mean.

January 7, 2009

On the road again. I am on the plane headed for Bangladesh. We were one hour late leaving, a real test of patience. We have been planning for weeks. This has been a good year. My friends at work got together and surprised me with $400 cash. I don't know who gave me the money. I wrote a thank-you note to everyone. People would asked me if I wanted to know. I would tell them that I didn't want to know, that way I would think nice thoughts about all of them. I put a sign up at work and collected Beanie babies, books, vitamins, Tylenol, Motrin, and surgical supplies. The hospital was getting rid of its pulse ox machines and I got three. One went *to Dr. Mac. She was grateful. I feel like I have been collecting things for a long time. Sarah B gave us $100. This money went for two computers; all together we are taking eight laptop computers, not bad. It's been a week of packing and unpacking. It was hard to give up things because we worked so hard collecting these things. Our group is Dr. Lee, Eun Soo Lee, Dr. Pak, Dr. Myung Shin, Dr. Eon Shin, Eun Jin Lee, Hong ,Spiritual Coach Dan, Toots, Connie, Dr. Young, Peter, Alex, Kim, and Rick. Yes, Rick is on the plane with me. He will be working on computers. He is not sure what he will do, but he is with us. He is now becoming part of our group. Connie will be meeting us in Singapore.*

We are not sure what we are going into. There has been an election in Bangladesh, and there was a travel advisory for Americans going to Bangladesh till January 5. I'm glad President Bush is still in office as we make this trip. I'm also glad that I have been there before; I have fewer nerves. Our lives have been very busy. Our grandchildren continue to grow. Alyssa turned thirteen years old on Sunday. We had a family party for her. Gibson is now twenty months. He is so cute, and we are enjoying him. Mark has a girlfriend; she is really nice and fits in our family. My job has been difficult, because of the auto industry slowdown, and we are seeing a decrease in patients, plus they over hired. We had two vacations days taken from us. We are also being cancelled a lot. We can take Excused Absent (EA: without pay) or Combined Time Off (CTO: our vacation time). This is hard on me because I want to do more of this kind of work and need to have vacation time. They are also forcing us to go to a twelve-hour shift, which means seventy-two hours of pay. This is a pay cut. All of this is a challenged, but at least I have a job. I am also grateful to be on this journey. I feel that God works on me because of this. I am not sure of what he wants but I will do it. I'm being nominated for the Nightingale Award. This is hard for me to take, but if it helps the people of Bangladesh, I will accept it. I'm so grateful to Dr. Sang Lee for his support. More later.

January 9, 2009, Day 2

We arrived in Singapore last night late 0030, after nineteen and a half hours of flying, pretty grueling. I slept a little on the plane. The second part of the trip was easier than the first. We had a plane with TVs in the seats, except Rick and I couldn't work the video games, neither one of us. After we got to the hotel, we had a burst of energy. We saw all the shops with food and had to eat. Dr. Lee had blood chicken soup. Dan had turtle soup. The rest of us had spring noodles. It was fun. I ended up spending the night with Toots and Eun Jin. Rick spent the night with Dr. Pak. I always enjoy being with Toots and Eun Jin. Rick and Eun Jin got up early and walked to the ocean. We woke up about 0745 after going to bed at 0400. I was still tired but Toots, Rick, Eun Jin, and Dr. Pak were raring to go. We had a buffet breakfast with fruit, noodles, and dim sum. The hotel is nice, next to a golf course. It has a beautiful pool but I didn't bring my suit.

We went to a market; I could have bought a suit but couldn't reason doing that with five or six suits at home. Rick and I went to the ocean for a walk (Changi Park). We watched the fishermen bringing in their catch. They would bring them in and put them on ice. Singapore is beautiful: green, palm trees, flowers everywhere, clean. They speak English and drive on the other side of the road. The people here seem happy, friendly, but look more Indian than Chinese, like I thought. I guess I have so much to learn about the world. When you're young, you think you know everything, but as you age, you know you don't. We went to a market; I think I found a rug for the family room. I don't think Rick likes it. It's hot here in Singapore and humid but beautiful. The group took a walk to the beach. I was sure glad I didn't shower because I was hot after. We talked a lot and really enjoyed being with each other. After we came back I took a bath in the tub that felt so good. Rick, Dan, and I ate Japanese food at the market; it was good.

Now we are the airport waiting for the flight to Dhaka. One thing I forgot to add on January 7 was that Rick's sister Shar gave us $40 for the trip, saying, "That's all the American money I had." [Rick's sister lives in Canada.] I felt like I was begging on Christmas Eve but I know what this means for the people. I sometimes wish I could do more but I will keep trying. We are on the plane to Dhaka and I'm starting to get nervous because I know what this means. A nice young lady is sitting across from me and keeps staring at me; I keep smiling and acknowledging her. The plane in Singapore Air; the seats are nice. Rick and I have no one between us, so we have lots of *room. The plane also has more educated and wealthier people on it. Seeing them reminds me why we are going. We joked last night about staying in Singapore and doing a service work for the poor. I know that there is work to be done there, as I saw a lady of the night walking last night, just like there is much work in Michigan, but we were called on this trip.*

January 10, 2009

We are in Dhaka. We were the last to go through customs. When we arrived, we got mixed up just as we were to go through. Connie and Toots were also there. It took an hour to go through; there were only a few customs officials. Good thing I didn't have to go to the bathroom. We watched the rest of the group struggle. Dr. Young had his first experience with not filling out the papers correctly. Alex was hit the hardest. I watched as it took a long time for him to go through. Dr. Lee waited on the other side of the glass. Dan had taken Alex's bag, drawing attention to Alex, as he didn't know. Alex was detained but by the grace of God went through. Rick was stopped but they asked if he was American and let us go.

January 11, 2009

Ten minutes to go. The ride from Dhaka was long and hard. Once again I am reminded why I am here. I saw Rick looking out the window. He is amazed by it all. We unpacked and there was chaos. I will go to eat now and will write later. Our morning meetings are very important and spirit filled.

January 11, 2009, Later

We were so busy today. Things started a little hectic at first, but I was more confident and felt more in charge. We have a local nurse named Purion, who is helping me. She has been a nurse for less than a year. She is a good nurse but needs direction. The other local nurses seem happier this year. I think they have been split up, plus they know we see their value. My friend Mrs. Cushim is still here. It was so good to see her. She is taking leadership in the group and looked different, more mature. She was happy to see me.

I was able by sign language to explain to patients what to do. That worked most of the time. We had a hard time starting IVs again, their veins are so tiny and they are so nervous, so it's hard. We had quite a scare. All of a sudden, there was a crash! It sounded like something had broken. Alex had kicked a soccer ball into the window. One of the workers was sitting there. Thank God he wasn't hurt. We had glass all over. We had a patient with bare feet; I found a broom and cleaned it up. Alex apologized a number of times. We had a good laugh about it.

When I wrote this, I wrote it as a matter of fact. I was in a different room at the time when I heard the loud crash. This noise scared me and scared the team in the OR because we did not see what happened. I thought that it was gun fire. The two workers sitting there were the men who would help carry the patient after the operation and would get supplies for us. Alex was there teaching soccer, a game he loved, so he was excited and hit the ball too hard. One thing that amazed me was that the next day, we saw the local workers putting up fishing net to protect the windows and the buildings. This took only a matter of a few hours, and we didn't have to go through committees and lots of talking. They saw the need and just did it. This reminded me of the creativity and imagination of the people here. I really have respect for these people.

One day as I was on the roof of our building, I saw Madame Chung coming back from town by rickshaw. I yelled to Dr. Young about this and told him he should do this. He took my advice and, without asking anyone else, hired a rickshaw driver to take him outside the compound. When he came back, he told me this was not a good idea, as the driver wanted to impress him and was going fast. The driver rounded the corner and Dr. Young fell out of the rickshaw. Thank God he was not hurt, and he has a story to tell.

January 12, 2009

I was too tired to finish writing yesterday. We are still seeing lots of prolapsed uteruses and doing repairs. The medical and pediatric teams are seeing many things. Dr. Myung Shin sent a child over with a hemangioma. The child was barely alive. I could hear his final breaths, and his coloring was poor. The mother was bottle feeding him; he was about nine months old. The mother would not leave till she saw Dr. Lee. We tried to tell her there was nothing we could do. This child required months of intensive care and a tracheotomy, which we could not do.

We also saw a woman who probably broke her leg a year ago and had massive cellulitis, probably osteomyelitis. We had to sent her away and told her she had to go to the hospital.

Once again I find that my words don't describe the feelings on seeing these people and knowing that there is nothing we can do; if we try, we can do more harm and may cause death. I never described the look this mother had as she held her child, desperately looking for help for him. When I saw him, I knew what we were facing because I had taken care of a few children with this type of abnormalities at Children's Hospital. I knew what kind of care would be required, and we couldn't give that care. As a mother, I knew that she knew this was her last hope for him. I knew that Dr. Lee would want to help this child and for a brief moment saw him trying to figure out how to help. I reminded him that we could not risk operating on this child. As a professional, I think you learn what you can and can't do, but you never lose the desire to want to help and try to figure out how you can. Soo and Madame Chung did pray over this mother and child and tried to give the mother emotional support.

January 13, 2008

Very busy day! We started the day good, things working well. We did rounds, and then we started. We saw lots of women with prolapes. We saw two young women with prolapses, one with two babies. We had a patient from yesterday who was bleeding. We had to do a repair in the recovery room. Dr. Lee put sutures in. She was really traumatized by it all. I had this patient and a post-op patient. We had to call Toots out of OR. Dr. Pak had to restart her IV and gave Versed. We later saw her, and she was still bleeding. We will take her back to OR in the morning. This is so hard because in the States she would have gone back right away, but we couldn't get into this OR and had no staff. I prayed for her tonight. We have been doing readings and meetings in the morning and night. We have been working on the reading from Mark about the mother, sister, and brothers. I realized that these people, these women, are my sisters. It's hard when we can't help them. I realize that when they say how hard their life is. They complain about stomach pain. We had a discussion with the medical team. Dr. Myung Shin had a patient, a young boy who was complaining of stomach pain. After she was going to give him medicine, she asked about meals and discovered that he only had one meal per day, so his pain was related to hunger. This may be what these women are going through.

Boy eating lunch in Bangladesh

The discussion we had about the little boy was hard on all of us, but it hit Dr. Shin hardest. She had been a pediatrician for many years and was surprised by this. We all know that there is hunger in United States, but when you see how these people live, you know it's not the same. We often say, "We are starving." We don't have a clue. Bangladesh is a country that has water and is green but they have lots of people, poor politics, and a lack of machinery. In all my visits and in all the time I spent looking out the window, I have only seen a handful of old tractors for the crops. Most of the farming is done by hand with old tools. We do so much complaining, but we have so much. I do forget this and complain myself till God takes me back to Bangladesh to remind me of my blessings.

January 13, 2009

It was a better day today, except Purion quit (or was fired), so things were hard on me. I'm still having a hard time with IVs, which makes everything harder, but Dr. Pak has been helping me. The women who was bleeding went to OR, but they found no reason for her bleeding. They did a D&C, and her bleeding stopped, and we were able to send her home. Thank you, God. I like being able to make decision but I do ask the doctors first, because that's how nurses do things.

This morning, Dan sang "Yes, Jesus Loves Me." And we sang "How Great Thou Art." Dan is a good speaker; he has a gift. I have been asked to talk tomorrow and I'm nervous. I think I will be focusing on Matthew 19: 13-14(NIV) ("Then little children were brought to Jesus for him to place his hands on them and pray for them. But the disciples rebuked those who brought them. Jesus said, 'Let the little children come to me, and do not hinder them for the kingdom of heaven belongs to such as these.'") I'll write tomorrow and tell you how it went. As I write this, the chanting is going on, only I think this is not the call to prayer but propaganda. We have government people around the compound, making sure we are okay. We didn't have devotions tonight. We needed to have some fun, so Eun Jin arranged a funeral for Alex's nipples with a death certificate signed by all of us. A eulogy was given by Dr. Lee, and Dan said prayers. We had a book to sign. We all laughed so hard, it was a good time. I am tired and we will do six operations tomorrow. Rick is downstairs talking. He is really enjoying himself and is being helpful to the people. Hong, Eun Jin, and I had a nice talk with Peter; he knows more about Detroit than I do.

I don't think anyone reading this will know what I was talking about. Alex will kill me for revealing his secret, but here goes (I love you, Alex): Dr. Lee happened to look at the back of Alex's neck and noticed two auxiliary nipples. Dr. Lee told Alex he could remove them. We joked about how Alex was in Bangladesh and no one would know, not even his wife. Sorry, Alex. Alex agreed to having surgery and we treated him like one of our patients. He had an IV and sedation, and we had a great time with this. Eun Jin made a coffin for his nipples. Alex was surprised by all of this but was a good sport. We would all have a good laugh about this. You could tell we enjoyed being together by the laugher. Alex's nipples were buried in Bangladesh, so part of him remains there.

January 14, 2009

It's early in the morning. I slept well but woke up early. I felt good but all of a sudden had a bout of nausea and a headache. I had to lie down. I thought, ***How will they do it? We are so busy****. I did talk this morning though. I think I did fine. I felt the spirit while I was speaking, but I think I stopped too quickly. We are a team and are acting as a team. The day went better. We finished at 1638. I joked with Sang about finishing at 1630. The local nurse, Purion, was back. I was happy to see her; her attitude was better. I find her warm but young. She had a much better attitude. She is very good at IV starts. She is more willing to share. She did go in to see OR. She reminds me of a teenager with a rebellious spirit. I'm starting to see more organizing with people. Rupal was thinking about what to use for IVs when we ran out of tubing. He is a curious man but has been sickly. Dr. Young gave him some Pepcid, and that seemed to help him fell better.*

A very scary thing happened when I gave a shot to a young women we were going to do a simple operation on. She walked from one room to the next and was doing fine. She was sitting in a chair, and all of a sudden, she was unresponsive. My first thought was that she had a severe allergic reaction and was going to die. I had given her penicillin, and because of language, I had no way of knowing if she was allergic. I was so scared and saw us all dying because of us hurting someone. I finally looked at her and realized she just fainted. Where is ammonia when you need it? The reason I didn't think she had fainted was the reaction was so delayed. I mean, she walked from one room to another. From that time on, Dr. Pak made sure I had ammonia at hand.

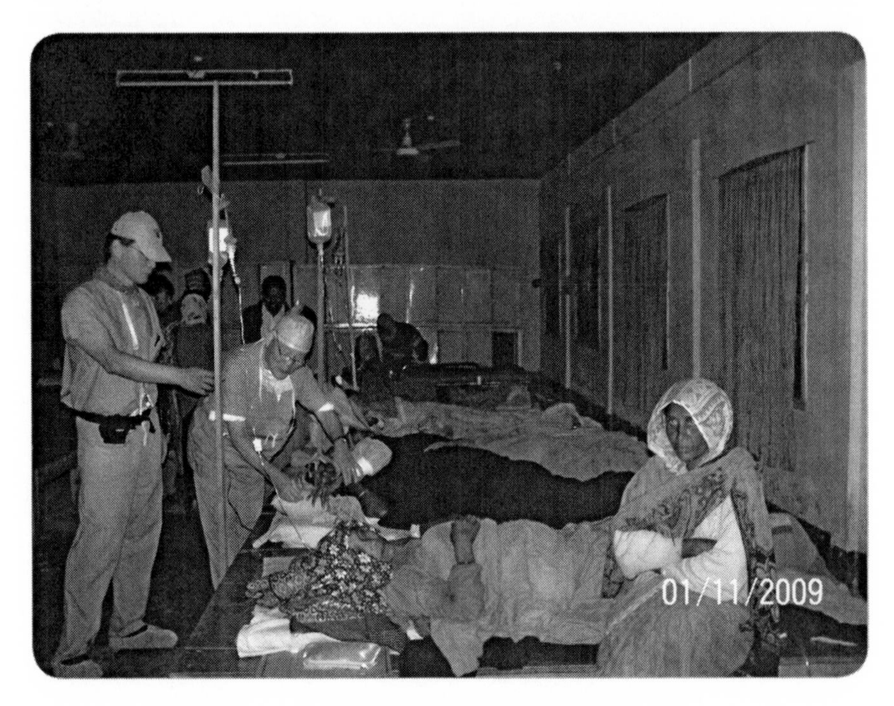

Dr. Lee and Dr. Pac making rounds

January 15, 2009

So many patients! Our days at the clinic, we see so many different things. We started the day with only four surgeries and ended with five. One patient was the worst of the prolapes. I felt sorry for her. The women really suffer with this. It's hard to see this. We had to turn a boy with a tumor away. I cried because of it. But it's time to go. We are getting tired and need to rest. We went to the island and saw what is going on there. We examined a patient who had no periods (only two in several years). Sang asked me to check her for pubic hair, she had none and small breasts. Dr. Lee said she had gonads but no uterus , meaning she was half woman and had the hormones of a man. We did not tell her because her husband would have left her. I noticed a baby with hydrocephalus but there is no way to tell. Hong and Peter left us. They flew back; it feels strange without them, like we are missing something. After we went to the island, we talked and sorted supplies for next time. We also checked the patients. They are doing well. Purion is staying with them tonight; it's good for her. We have packed up, and in the morning we will be leaving. It's hard leaving, and it will be hard saying good-bye to Miss Chang and Madame Yoo and Director Chang. When we get to Singapore, we will be split again, but I feel my spirit will always be with them. They have become my brothers and sisters in life. Will I come back here? I hope so, God willing.

I was shocked when Sang felt this woman and said she had gonads; I thought I heard him wrong. Gonads, a woman? He then explained that she had no uterus, and the gonads could develop into cancer and needed to be removed. She was our last patient we were seeing for the day. He instructed Mrs. Cushim not to tell her what he found, knowing that she would be rejected by her husband; he promised to see her next year and to tell Miss Chang of her plight so that she could be helped. This woman was about twenty-five years old and came to see us because she was not able to get pregnant. Once again, if this woman had access to medical care, this would have been found out years ago, and she would have been helped.

The trips to the islands are as important for us as the medical care, because we get to see first hand how our patients live and what they are up against. The boats have no motors. Life on the islands is primitive, and to quote Director Chang, these are "disappearing islands." Director Chang is always teasing us about selling us one of these islands. Here today, gone tomorrow. These are the areas where flooding occurs, from the melting of the snow off the Himalayas in India. Alex made a comment about how many large cities (Chicago, Detroit, New York, London) have water and port access, so he saw this as potential for this area. Alex is a visionary. Director Chang saw this also.

January 16, 2009

It's early in the morning. We are leaving. Everything is rushed. Our reading this morning touched me; it was about Jesus chasing out the spirit. Just a reminder of what we are up against. We made rounds this morning. The lady with the bad prolapse case. I had Sang and Young take a picture with her. She smiled again. Once again I say good-bye to Madame Chang and Madame Yoo. I will miss these saints and will continue to pray for them. The trip home is long. I pray to God we make it safe. I do look at these people differently; my sisters in the world suffer, and my brothers in the world suffer. The children of the world suffer. Their answer is not what money can buy. They need hope for their future and their children's future. God, I will do whatever you want me to do. Use me in the way you want to. Dan said that even in the United States, my sisters suffer, my brothers suffer. I will do what you want. Thank you, God, for this trip!

One of the things you don't expect when you do this work is gifts. The workers don't have much, but just like us, they are proud people and want to give back. Most of the workers are Muslims but know that we are Christians, and they want to give to us. Just before we left we were presented with the gift of a wooden cross. I cannot begin to tell you what that gift meant to me. The cross is beautifully made and sits on my desk. Both Rick and I received this cross. Every time I see the cross, it reminds me of Bangladesh, and my heart goes back there.

The thoughtfulness of this gift goes beyond words that I can describe.

January 16, 2009

A lot happened since this morning! About two hours into the trip, we were in a car accident. Director Chang was driving. We had a head-on crash in our car. We were all shaken up. Connie was instantly crying, "My leg, my leg." Dr. Eon Shin looked pale. Dr. Myung Shin was okay. The other driver came over to us right away and noticed Dan; his head and arm were bleeding. Director Chang was okay. I was doing fine till I stepped down and then felt pain in my leg and neck. My blouse was open when we got off the bus. We decided not to wait for an ambulance, which was a good decision. We all fit into one van. Connie kept saying, "My leg, my leg." Dr. Lee sat with her and talked to her. We prayed and then sang "I Love You, Lord" and "I Lift My Voice."

In the van, Alex started singing "I Love You, Lord," the song that we practiced to sing to the people in Bangladesh, and we sing in three languages in the Korean church. We practice this song and have sung this song many times together, so it binds us together. Singing the song at that time relaxed all of our spirits after what had just happened. I want to share the words of this song with you:

I Love You, Lord

I love you. Lord, and I lift my voice
Bal lo ba si On ddu ran di e

To worship you, Oh my soul rejoice
Bbu ro nam ko ree Ah mal bburan sooke

Take joy, my King, In what you hear.
Ah mal la jiah Ah mal balio basha

May it be a sweet, sweet sound
Ddo mal gganne shundol shundol

In your ear.
Shuniae jai.

January 17, 2009

I was too tired on the plane to finish what went on. I slept on the plane. Dr. Eon Shin had a dislocated right arm. He knew instantly that he had dislocated it. How brilliant he was in diagnosis. Dr. Myung Shin was in shock but did well till later and had lots of pain in her left leg. Dan has a broken left leg and glass in his foot. Sang took it out and put sutures in. Both Dan and I were put in a cast. I thought they were putting an ace bandage on but they cast my ankle. We ended up at a nearby hospital and were seen by a doctor. Connie had a left femur facture. I had a left ankle sprain. I had to go to the bathroom without a wheelchair, and these beautiful Bangladesh women helped me to the bathroom. I was in so much pain and didn't want these little ladies helping me, this big woman. The bathroom was a long way. Rick and Soo also helped. They took us to an x-ray room. I have never seen such a dark and dirty room, but they got the x-ray. Sang and Dr. Eon Shin saw all the x-rays and we got copies. They put Connie and me in a room and catheterized Connie. She wanted Toots to do it. She wanted all of the men out. She was so scared. I kept holding her hand and talking to her. Toots was not able to get the Foley in. I think she was still shaken by what had happened. Connie was still worried about the men in the room. Dr. Lee came but the local doctor put the Foley in. The local doctor was a very nice man. People helped me. There was a difference, men could help a woman. As I was sitting in the wheelchair waiting for my x-ray, everyone was around me looking at what had happened. As soon as we knew our injuries, we made plans to get Connie to the hospital in Dhaka. Connie did not want to go there. We wanted to get her on the plane and operate in the United States. Alex and Dr. Lee tried for hours to get that to happen. Because she needed a stretcher to be transported and the airlines did not have one, this could not be done, so she was operated on in Dhaka. Alex had called the embassy for recommendations. They had to get an OR ready.

I remember this accident like it was yesterday. I was grateful that I had my i-Pod playing Christian music and my eyes closed so I did not see what happened. I had rested my leg on the wheel cover so my ankle took the force of the crash. The trip in the van has always made me nervous, so I play music and keep my eyes closed at times. Rick was not so lucky, as he saw the accident. Toots also saw the accident; this would be hard on her, as she has had family members who died in car accidents. Connie was asleep and fell right off the seat, hitting the seat ahead of her. Rick and I were in the last seat. I had not wanted to go in this van when we were leaving Chilmary and headed for the other van, but the director told me I would be more comfortable in this van so I went.

We were about two hours into our trip. Director Chang was driving our van. My understanding of what happened was that we were passing another car when we were hit. We were blessed that we did not go over the edge of the road, as the road was narrow. I will never forget Dr. Shin saying, "Let's call for an ambulance." There would be no ambulances. We then were surrounded by the local people. The driver of the truck ran away, I guess afraid of what was going to happen to him. After much thought it was decided that we should all get into the other van. Thank God we were on the return trip, because we had no supplies. Deciding how we would move Connie was a challenge. But God would provide. A local person just happened to come by with a cart that was the right height. Dan would later tell me that he moved his leg and there was just a perfect space so that he could take his leg out of the car without cutting it. Dan and the director were the only people who had a seat belt on, and to this day I feel that they would have died that day without it.

As we sat in the van, all of us started to have lots of pain, especially Connie. We sang and then we realized that we had left all the supplies back at Chilmary, so we looked for solutions. We had brought supplies and medicine to the people, and our work was done; we never expected that we would need medicine. I happened to have an unopened bottle of Motrin, so we passed that around for pain. The director drove our van to the hospital. I made it sound like it was a short trip, but it was about two hours. We had to go over the one-way bridge. This bridge is the hardest of the trip. It is a wooden bridge that has planks that are uneven, making the ride full of bumps. Every bump we went over caused Connie more pain. Hearing her cries was so painful for all of us; we were helpless to make this pain better. Director Chang could be heard sighing as Connie moaned. Driving us to the hospital must have been very challenging for him because he was the driver and was hit, but he was the only one who knew the roads and spoke the language.

When we got to the hospital, we had other experiences. We were treated well but there was much confusion. I had to hop to get around, and of course I had to go to the bathroom, thus my diary entry about the women helping me. We did see someone bleeding in the emergency room. Connie was taken back and had her x-ray first. Finally Dan and I got wheelchairs and we were taken to the x-ray room. While I was waiting for my x-ray, I noticed that the local people were looking at me and Alex, probably wondering what this Korean man was doing with this Caucasian woman. I told Alex that we would show them that we loved each other with the love of Jesus. After the x-ray, I was taken to Connie's room; that would be the last time I saw Connie for a few months. My leg was put in a cast, and then I was taken back to the van.

We waited and waited. It was decided that Connie would be taken to Dhaka for surgery, but she would be taken in an ambulance with an air conditioner for some comfort. Dr. Lee, Soo, Toots, and Dr. Pak would ride with her. An IV was started so she could be given IV pain medications. I would find out later that the supplies we used, pain medications, Foley, IVs, and casting materials, were not available to us and were purchased for us. One of the workers from Chilmary heard about the accident and came to the hospital to see us. It was so good to see him. The people we had left were worried about us and wanted to see if they could help. God does bind people together for his purpose.

The ride back was long; we did not stop for lunch, since we had a flight to catch and Connie had to get to the hospital. The director drove our van. I don't know how he did that, being he was in the car and had to be feeling sore and pain and guilty. He drove till we met one of the workers. It was already dark by this time. Because he knew we would be getting hungry, he had grabbed some oranges, which we shared. We did stop once for a bathroom stop. Driving in Dhaka was the worst: lots of traffic, lots of stop and go. The trip was so long and hard that Dr. Young became car sick and started throwing up, but we could not stop so he threw up out the window. The sound of him being sick was hard and reminded me that we all went through the accident with each other, those in the van and those who saw the accident.

When we arrived at the airport, once again there was confusion. We had to hurry to catch the plane; Alex had called the airport to hold the plane. Soo and Sang got out of the ambulance to say good-bye, as they had decided to stay with Connie for a few days till she was settled.

Leaving them, especially leaving Connie there, was hard. The Bible talks about how the body of Christians are one body with many parts. When we were leaving, it felt like part of my body was injured with Connie. Leaving her there and not seeing her was so hard. I cried. We hugged. The director kept saying to me, "I'm sorry." I hugged him and told him I loved him and we would see each other again. Then we got through customs and on the plane. I tried to get on the plane by hopping; I hopped up and ended up stepping on my foot and felt terrible pain.

I would later hear that it took an hour or so to get Connie to the hospital because the driver stopped along the way. I was also told that Dr. Sang and Dr. Pak held Connie's hip the whole time during the trip to Dhaka. The doctor in Dhaka who operated on Connie told Dr. Lee, "Your God must love Connie very much." My life will be always changed as a result of this accident. I really saw what local people lived with. When they are sick, where do they go for care? Out of that accident came our desire to build a hospital in Chilmary. This has been a long project, very slow moving. The reason I am writing this book is for the hospital. A real hospital, not just a room converted into an OR.

January 18, 2009

We are on the plane home. The last leg of our journey together. Rick was able to get wheelchairs for us, but it took all day. We called at 1000 and didn't get the chair till 1600. I had to stay in the room till then; I crawled to my knees to get to the bathroom. This makes things challenging, but at least I have my knees. Dan does not have that. He came in my room and talked. He needed to talk things out. Our Scripture reading was on healing, and he found that interesting. I told him how I found it amazing that two days before, he had talked about dying. He is still processing how close he came. Because Rick was able to get the wheelchairs, we were able to get out of the hotel room and see some of Singapore. We went to the market. We bought some washcloths, mushrooms, scallops, nuts, candy, and ice cream from a stand. We walked past two Buddhist temples. We saw some people praying and offering incense. Rick was bothered by the temples.

We had been told that Singapore had cheap electronics but couldn't find an electronics store, so we couldn't find anything for Rick. We really couldn't find anything for the kids. The market was crowded, and it was hard to move with the wheelchair. I was glad that Rick pushed me around. The hotel we stayed in was cheap for a reason. Lots of call girls with the travelers. We could see it all night. The room was small with a plastic mattress. We keep our complaining to a minimum after what we had been through. I was grateful for a bed.

We had just made the plane in Dhaka, so no down time. At least in Singapore we have twenty-four hours. Alex saw his friend and will be staying with him. Dr. Shin, Eun Jin, Dr. Young, and Dr. Pak went to the market. And later we all went to eat at a restaurant called Jumbo Seafood. The food was good, and we enjoyed each others' company and felt the love we have for each other. For months we have been thinking of ourselves as a team. We walked in a park and saw a jump board course and watched people jump boarding. Then we went back to sleep for three or four hours. I am in a wheelchair now, as I don't want to bear any weight till I see my doctor. I will know tomorrow what I can and can't do. The wheelchair is no fun; people have to push you around, and if you try yourself, your arms hurt. To get Dan and me on the plane, we needed a special wheelchair, like a lift. The workers have you sit in it and pull you backwards. On our flight from Singapore to Tokyo, I was in row 11, so the bathroom was a long way back; they had to get the lift for me twice. How embarrassing it was for everyone to know when you go to the bathroom, but the staff was so nice about it. The one flight attendant was so friendly and never complained. That is nice for Northwest.

Right now, I am in row 67. This is close to the bathroom but hard for me to see the TV, but the bathroom is more important. I wish I could share everything but that would be impossible. The memories, the aroma, the sights. I need to make amends to Dan the way I acted yesterday. When Alex, Dr. Shin, and Dr. Young had a beer, we said, "Let's put the beer in front of Dan and take a picture." I was right there too. But Dan explained that for him being a holy man, this was not right. It might cause others to fall. It was something I hadn't thought about.

The journey is almost over. We are an hour away from home. My leg is hurting again. I thought I was doing better, but I went to the bathroom just now and felt more pain. I'm thinking of Connie in a strange country, having surgery. How hard it must be for her. We need to keep praying for her. When I think of the trip, I think pleasant thoughts. We did a lot of good. All of us knew the price we could pay, and some of us have. God, we love you. God, we accept your will. I am so grateful for all I have and where I live. I am so grateful for my friends. I am grateful for the people of Bangladesh for all they have taught me. I will always remember the singing, the morning routine, and the children saying, "Morning, madam." I will always remember the women who want to tell me their story, and the smiles after. I don't think any of us would trade that. I don't know your purpose, Lord, but I will accept it. I think because of the devotions and time spent together, Rick and I are closer, quite closer.

Some of the funny things I remember about Singapore was how I got up to the room. Remember, I had a cast on my leg and had to hop. It was a long way, so the hotel decided that I would get on dolly and be pushed from the elevator to our room. What a sight! Dan also had to go up the same way. Alex's friend had told us about this hotel, and we picked it for price. When we got to the hotel, we realized what kind of hotel it was. Dr. Young tried to tell Eun Jin, but she became annoyed with him and wouldn't listen, so we were staying there. To this day, we laugh and tease Eun Jin because of this.

Getting the wheelchairs proved to be much harder than we thought. It took the company all day to get it, and when they came, they would not accept a credit card, so Rick had to find an ATM to give him $1,000 cash (most of it was held as a deposit). Dr. Eon Shin went to a clinic to have his arm set. After that, instead of getting some much needed rest, he decided to go on a tour of Singapore. He tried to get Dr. Pak, Eun Jin, Toots, Dr. Young, and Dr. Myung Shin to go with him, but no one would go, so he went by himself and was happy he went. He shared some of the information he learned with us. We still laugh about this. Before this trip, I kept telling my friends at work how excited I was to be visiting Singapore. One of the lessons I learned by sitting and waiting for a wheelchair (while my husband and friends were sightseeing!) was not to brag about my travels. You see, I kept saying I couldn't wait to see Singapore and stay there for twenty-four hours. I kept saying what I was going to do, like I was in control of the trip. I forgot the part in the Bible which says if God wills it, I will do it. Thanks, God, for the reminder of who is in control.

January 21, 2009

We are home. I am still feeling a little jet lag. Update: I have a torn ligament in my left leg. I went to the doctors Monday; I have a walking brace, which I am grateful for. I get four weeks off work. I'm not in pain, but I am still swollen, and everything takes longer. I have made three trips to the store. I can't bring the groceries into the house. I am already bored, but I'm trying to make the best of it. Connie remains in Bangladesh. According to Soo, she is in a nice hospital, doing well. They have found some Filipino nurses and doctors. Dr. Lee gave her a cell phone so she could call people. She will be there for four to six weeks.

Dr. Lee and Soo are back home. I haven't seen them yet but Soo has talked to Rick. We heard from Eun Jin that Dan does not have a break or a head injury. What a miracle! Rick and I were sharing at Bible study about our experiences, and he reminded me about the chants we heard in Chilmary the first night we were there. We heard chants about 0200. I was able to fall asleep in spite of it. Rick said when they stopped it was like the "sound of silence." At times we would hear the voices surrounding the compound. In spite of this, we never felt any fear. We felt joy and peace.

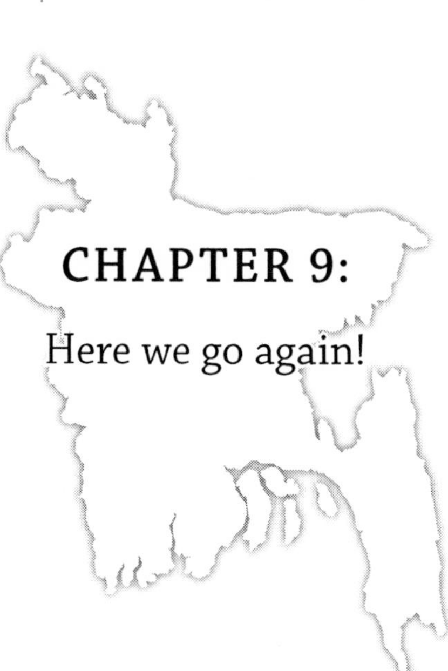

CHAPTER 9:

Here we go again!

February 1, 2011

On the road again. It's hard to believe we are on a plane to Bangladesh. Rick is on the plane with me. What a busy few weeks. I love being with these people. The group consisted of Dr. Sang Lee, Eun Soo Lee, Dr. Pak, Dr. Catherine Stark, Toots, Connie, Mr. Kim, Gu Jae Kwon, Eun Jin, and Chong-Hui Koo. What a day yesterday was. We were scheduled to leave tomorrow, but because they are predicting a large snowstorm, we are leaving today. We had some anxiety yesterday as Sang, Toots, and myself were working. Dr. John Lee was also working. John could not get the day off. I almost did not get the day off. Kathy, my boss, said if I could find coverage, I could go. I was in the circumcision room when Sang came and told me they were leaving today to get out before the storm. I went and asked Lisa Delia and Kim Marasco to work for me in front of Kathy and Sang; they both agreed to work but Kathy was unsure, but because of Sang and the girls' presence, she brought the papers into the room and we signed them.

The reason we were in the hallway is that Sang wanted the pulse oximetry machine that I got from respiratory therapy. I am so lucky to have such friends that they would help me like that. We will bring them back something. Lisa wasn't happy but did it. [Thank you, Lisa.] Then I called Rick. Sang and Soo called the airlines, and we were flying standby. Toots called Rick, asking why we weren't going with her on Wednesday, as planned. He called me at work, and I told him to let Soo and Sang handle this. I prayed that

Toots would be with us. I had the feeling when I was walking out of work that she would be with us. When I got home, Rick said that Soo called and Toots was going with us.

I'm not sure what God's plan is in this, but I know that he is guiding us. Rick and I rushed to finish packing and were a little testy with each other, but we got everything done. Right after I talked to Sang, I felt the peace that I have been having about this trip leaving me. I felt anxious but still knew that God was in charge. I took extra blood pressure medicine, feeling like my blood pressure was up. I was able to sleep. I am glad that Rick is going with us. I'm not sure the kids are glad. I turned sixty on January 24, 2011; it's hard to believe that I'm sixty. The girls at work gave me a party. Dr. Mac saw the sign up and ordered Pancit and egg rolls. She did this even though she wasn't going to be there. I was so touched. That was so sweet. I am so lucky and blessed. I have doctors that I call my friends.

I worked till 3 pm on my birthday. Prudi brought me a cake and everyone sang. I am really lucky that the people I work with treat me so well. I received cards and calls from my family. We went to Frankenmuth and spent the night at Splash Mountain. I just wanted to be with my kids and grandchildren. We had fun, except Gibson was afraid of the pools (he was tired), and Brittany had a panic attack. I learned something about Brittany: she does not do well in a new place. I'm hoping when we go to Italy, she will outgrow this. The kids had fun. Alyssa told me she couldn't buy me anything but she loved me. That evening, Gina painted my toenails blue. I felt like we were girlfriends. I also enjoyed being pampered. I am glad that we chose to spend time together as a family. As a child, I never had a family vacation, and it meant a lot to me. I hope that some day, the kids and grandchildren will see the value.

The next part of the diary is about what has happened in the last two years. I am still working on post partum at Troy Beaumont, still on the day shift. I still enjoy my job but do not like the twelve-hour shifts. Lots of walking, because Beaumont has put us on an exercise plan [this is a joke I'm trying to make], making us walk (about half a mile) from the parking lot, no more shuttle. Also we just started walking rounds. The half hour in the morning to sit is gone, and the half hour before going home is gone.

They tell us the patients like this. Whatever! Our granddaughter is fifteen years old now, along with our step-granddaughter. They are driving. Our grandson is three and a half and will be four in April. Gina was pregnant but the baby never formed, so that was a loss. Mark will finish with his BA in March. Because of the job market in Michigan, he is talking about going out of state for work. He is going to Texas in February to meet a girl he has been talking to. Rick lost his job a month after he turned sixty. He was let go and we took his pension buyout to invest it for ourselves. The loss of his job has been hard on both of us. He is trying to get an on-line business going. It can be hard on me because he gets to baby-sit and choose his own hours. I'm trying to stay positive, work hard, and stay in God's plan. My friend Joyce, who retired from Beaumont, is now volunteering on street patrol in Arizona; there is hope for me. Three things happened that really have impacted my life.

First, my cousin Hank died. He had cancer. He always treated me well and took us places. I stood up as a flower girl in Reggie and Hank's wedding. Both of them were such a part of my life. I felt a loss at his passing. I went to the funeral with my cousin Barb. I always enjoyed the time I spent with her.

Second, my friend Sharon's husband, Al, was in the hospital for open heart surgery. He had three procedures, was very sick, and died from complications. When he was sick, he did not want visitors, which made it hard. Sharon and Al were our traveling buddies: England, Hawaii, and Las Vegas. Rick and I were supportive of Sharon, but I hate seeing her in pain. She is moving on; she has sold her house, bought a new condo, and is keeping busy.

Third, the most painful, my cousin Barb died of a massive heart attack at fifty-seven. She went to work, did not feel good, lay down, and died. Barb was more like a sister to me. Her death has taught me so many things. I know what it means to live in the day. Make plans but don't plan outcomes. This is what the slogan "One day at a time" means. I also am so grateful for the twelve-step program, because I think that part of why my cousin died was because of someone's drinking. We say that alcoholics die, go crazy, or recover. And nondrinkers can go through the same things. Barb and I were best friends growing up. We did so many things together. In high school, we had classes together. We worked at K-Mart together, she stood up in my wedding, and she was Gina's godmother. After she met Ray, she didn't visit as much, but she would come when she could.

I gave the eulogy at her funeral. I am grateful that we went on a road trip to Florida. Barb loved that road trip so much. I think she felt peace for a little while. I would think I had to be doing something, and she would just look out the window and enjoy the view. After the trip we visited my sister Judy in Pennsylvania and got lost on the way home. Nothing can ever take those memories away. I keep reaching out to Barb's sons, but it's hard to reach them.

February 3, 2011

We arrived safe and sound. The flight from Detroit was long, and even though we are in the aisle, both Rick and I were unable to sleep. I watched movies, read, and wrote. We arrived about 0100 at Alex and Serena's beautiful three-story house. They are putting us up for two nights. We saw Singapore only by night. It's hot here, in the 80s and humid. I was so tired when we arrived. The men stayed at the airport to get the luggage from one terminal to the other. They said they walked the airport. I stayed up waiting for Rick; we were up till 0400. I slept well on an air mattress in Alex and Serena's room. This morning, Serena made us breakfast. We had morning devotions. We all said what we had been going through before we arrived. We said prayers with each other. We are becoming one. The prayers are so powerful. I love being with these people, but the purpose of this trip is the people of Bangladesh.

February 3, 2011, 1600

We went into downtown Singapore. What a sight: all different cultures. The new building with the boat on top was beautiful. We went for a ride on a river boat. It was so beautiful. We went under an old bridge; the water was green-brown, so probably not the best for swimming. I am sick. I'm having stomach pain, nausea, and diarrhea. I was able to make the cruise, but I was so glad we came home after. I am up in our room. I lay down for a few minutes. I hear everyone talking downstairs. I got bored so I started to write. What can I tell you about the people I am with? This is not written in the order of importance, and I do not want to make people upset. This is written with love and so readers will understand:

Dr. Sang Lee: a very tall and slender Korean man. Quiet by nature but speaks with authority. A very dry humor, highly respected by his peers. He is very spiritual. He works hard. I will forever be grateful to him for taking me on these adventures. He really didn't know me and took a chance.

Eun Soo Lee: Dr. Lee's wife. A lady with joy. She is beautiful, vivacious, full of energy, and a committed Christian. I love being with her. She is Korean but can relate with all cultures. She is fun with lots of energy. She thinks she does not have a place here because she is not medical, but she holds Sang and us together. She takes care of the money. [She makes sure we have enough money for the trip, a very important job.]

Toots (Celia Mateo): I love Toots. Our first meeting was at the Korean church, and I thought she was Korean. We still laugh because she is Filipino. She is a great cook, loves to travel. She came back from Antarctica last week. She is generous to a fault, thinks of others first, keeps the OR tidy. She is brave going on this trip because several of her family died in a car accident.

Connie Escrupolo: she is a retired OR nurse. Out of all of us, she is the bravest making this trip. She was the one who was hurt. She is so faithful to God. She has no fears about this trip. She is an example. She is always e-mailing me things that are beautiful.

Dr. Choon Whan Pak: he is a retired anesthesiologist. He is a gentle, quiet man who doesn't say much. He has doubt in his faith, but I see more peace in him. His wife and he are so loving and supportive of us. It is such a pleasure to work with him.

Gu Jae Kwon (Mr. Nine): he is younger than us but has gray hair. He speaks Korean but understands English. He will be working with Mr. Kim on repairing Mrs. Yoo's house. I am just getting to know him.

Chong: a Korean woman with three boys. She owns a dry cleaners. She is happy and fun. I had to laugh as she woke up last night at 0100, thought it was 0800, showered, dressed, put on makeup, and went downstairs. She woke up Alex and Serena and Eun Jin; what a laugh. She doesn't know why God called her here.

Mr. Kim: our leader. A quiet Korean man who is always looking out for us. He made copies of our passports. He made us goodies bags. He makes sure we are all there. This is my second trip with him, and it's a blessing to be in his care.

Dr. Catherine Stark: I have known Dr. Stark for some time. I liked her before. The funny thing is I've worked with her husband (Jay). Dr. Stark is a faithful Christian who loves God. We are sitting in the sun by a beautiful pool with a cascading fountain, very relaxing. Dr. Stark is warm, and we share some talk about our children. We also talk about weight loss.

Alex Kim: a young Korean man with a wife, Serena, and four beautiful children. This is my second trip with him. His family and he moved to Singapore six months ago for work. We keep saying that God put him here for us. We spent two days here in his house, relaxing. What a blessing. I am happy to see a godly family. Serena is always so willing to serve.

Eun Jin Lee: a young woman with lots of energy, wonderful organizational skills, and a joy to be around. She has been enjoying Alex's children since we arrived. Eun Jin loves God, loves people, and is a faithful servant. She inspires me and encourages me so many times.

Two other members that I did not write about but were part of the team:

Coach David Shin: He is from Taiwan, a holy man of the Korean church in Michigan. I like David as soon as I met him. He is full of energy and loves God. He has been in this church for about six months and is new to Michigan.

Dr. John Lee: He was the only one of us who did not make it out because of the storm. John is a pulmonologist. He is very bright, loves life, easy to talk to. He is fun to be around.

February 4, 2011

I woke up feeling better but still have a wave of nausea, which passes. I was able to eat breakfast. Serena made omelets, egg sandwiches, and hash browns. Our devotion was very meaningful. We sang, said prayers, and studied. We are trying to become one. Rick went to the market, and I swam. The pool is so beautiful, larger than I am used to. I was only able to swim seventy laps, and then I did water aerobics. I got a little sun. It was so relaxing. I am going to have a tan. I got back, ate, and then we left for the airport.

February 4,2011 1900

We are on the plane again. David is with us, but still no John. We made the right decision coming early. Singapore Airport is beautiful, like a mall. You don't go through security till you reach the gate; therefore, you can have your family come and see you off. The mall has lots of shops, lots of shops. I brought Mrs. Cushim some ache medicine; I wanted to do this before we left but never got around to it. While we were going through security, I saw some Bengali people and found myself passing judgment. I not sure where that comes from. I thought I was going to help, and I'm passing judgment. Bengali people are different but feel like I do: they love their families and want the same things I want. I notice more men in suits. Most of the people on the plane are the upper class of people, so that may be the reason for judgment. I'm asking God to remove the judgment from me. I want to be of service.

February 5, 2011

We arrived late last night. The flight was great. I watched the movie Secretariat. I enjoyed that very much. As soon as the plane touched down, I could see the smog. It smelled like smoke. Again confusion at the airport. It took a very long time for us to get through customs. Of course I picked the wrong line. We waited and waited. I went through the Bangladesh line because there was no one there. I could see Rick was worried about that. Confusion over the bags. Sang told people to take any bag. But Alex took my bag. Because of this, we were spotted and detained. I could see the director through the window. Finally he came in, and then the trouble started. They wouldn't let us go. We waited and waited, meanwhile the director was being hassled by local authorities. They went back and forth, back and forth. They wanted money. I could feel that the director was under great attack. I began praying with zeal and told others. Cathy was asking a lot of questions. Some local workers began talking and asking what was in our bags. She started to talk, but I stopped the conversation, not knowing if they were trustworthy. The director went back and forth three times. More waiting; we were tired. Finally the local authorities came over and apologized for the wait and welcomed us to Bangladesh.

Going out of the airport was easier than most times, less people at the gate. We were taken in a large bus to our hotel. The street again was full and noisy but traffic was better than usual, the smog heavy. Rick sat next to me. The director then welcomed us as Alex translated. They gave us juice and we went up to our rooms. Rick and I were able to sleep together and prayed together. The room is nice but bed and pillows hard. We talked, became tired, and fell asleep. I woke at 0600 without the call to prayer, surprise. We had a nice shower, went to breakfast, and are awaiting the journey. I am not feeling good.

One of the things I did not write about was how we were swarmed by the mosquitoes when we got off the plane; Soo made a comment to the stewards about keeping the mosquitoes out of the plane, and the stewards said that they were already on the plane. I wish I had my bracelets. Sure glad that I took medicine for malaria.

February 5, 2011, 0830

We are on the bus, a large luxurious bus by Bangladesh standards. We just found out that before we landed there was a 6.4 earthquake at 1930. We landed at 2100. This explains a lot of what we felt last night. I guess this is why we are here. Rick tried calling our children. Cathy is worried about Jay's concern.

I couldn't write any more because the bus was moving.

February 5, 2011, 2230

Director Chang didn't know about the earthquake. He didn't feel it. Madame Chang did feel it. The ride from Dhaka is long and hard on all of us. We went through many towns. We heard the honking of horns, sometimes continuously. I watch the people walking by the bus, and I see the chaos. I listen to my I-Pod to get through it. Rick took pictures. We went across the old bridge again, this should be the last year, as they are building a new one. The director shows us the spot where the accident occurred. Toots and Connie seem fine. No flashbacks for me. The director is so funny. There was a race going on, and he took his wallet and I think he paid off the police so we could go through. [This is my interruption; I was told that he would not do that because it only encourages that behavior.] *I hate the long ride. I feel a lot of stress on the trip. We arrive at Chilmary Medical Center when it was dark but we saw our old friends.* [It was more than just seeing old friends; the workers were waiting for our bus to arrive. It was dark and they could be at their homes, but they chose to meet our bus. We were all so excited to see each other. It felt like we were home. It felt like our family was greeting us.] *Then we ate with staff, good food, and unpacked. I think we have an order figured out; we will see how things go tomorrow. We had devotions, and now I'm sleepy. Rick and I are sleeping in the same room as last year.*

February 6, 2011

I woke up at 0400 with racing thoughts, trying to organize the plan for today. I asked Dr. Pak for help with IVs, we need a blood pressure machine, we need medicine labels. I asked Soo to help with that since there will be no clinic today. John is in Dhaka, on his way. We will finally be together. We had devotions, and it settled me down. I love being with these people. David is leading us in good devotions. I have asked for better directions and feel more confident. I have done this before, I am a good nurse, and God has prepared us.

February 6,2011 1830

We are done. It's been a busy day. We did seven cases. I feel better because we started about 0935. It's so good to see Mrs. Cushim. She is so beautiful, but she is not my translator. I have two new nurses to help me, so lots of teaching. Lots of scared women, lots of confusion, but better than in previous years. Cathy wants to interview everyone, which can slow down the process. I was unable to start IVs at first, but later in the day I was doing better. More joy, less chaos. We did seven operations, we were scheduled for nine but one woman was wheezing too much. She had a history of TB and said she had pneumonia. The second woman's blood pressure was 180/110, her family was crying. We are sending her to John, and he will evaluate whether we will operate on Wednesday. She hugged me on both sides of the face. I love getting to know the local people.

Language is a problem. I know we are making a difference, all of us. How God put all of us from different backgrounds together, I don't know. Sang hinted that there was some research money to build a women and children's hospital here. Wouldn't that be a miracle? Rick was able to do some good things with the computers. He said that eighteen guys were standing around a computer and connected to the Internet. Wow! I watched Alex playing soccer with the kids, what a sight. The director is so pleased. You can just see it in him. Madame Yoo and Madame Chang are also pleased. Madame Chang does not seem as rushed to serve as before, more relaxed, less stressed.

The lady with the elevated blood pressure was so sad because we were not going to do her surgery. She couldn't understand why because she was on blood pressure medicine. I explained through Mrs. Cushim that there would be risk to her having the surgery with her blood pressure being so high. I also shared with this patient that I had blood pressure issues and was taking two medicines a day to keep my blood pressure stable. Once this woman heard this, she understood and, though disappointed, went away knowing we cared about her.

We had a patient who came back from OR and started throwing up. She was still sedated. I turned her head so she threw up against the wall. Because of the size of the table she was on, it was safer to turn her that way. I was scared because we had no suction and she could aspirate and stop breathing. After a while she stopped, and then we moved her. Then we had emesis on the wall. The local people would not touch this, they were motioning for her family to clean this. I chose to help the family clean this up, showing compassion; this is not easy to do because we don't have the cleaning supplies we would have in the hospital. Once again I felt challenged by what I am called to do in Bangladesh.

February 7, 2011

We woke up early. I wake up trying to make things better. Then I realized that my blood pressure was going up. I decided to read, which helped. Cathy is finding it hard not to have a relationship with her patients. I know her feelings, but we can't do things the same here. The morning devotions are great. David is such a good teacher; it's great to hear his sermons.

February 7,2011 1919

We just finished dinner. I was hungry, as I missed my lunch. Everyone was worried but I have a late lunch many days without having a big breakfast. I surely will not starve without a meal. Connie gave her testimony this morning. It was wonderful. I found things out about Connie I didn't know. She talked about the accident and growing up. Everyone gave her a standing ovation. I was reliving the accident with her. That whole day can still bring tears to me. The rest of the day was busy, we got a late start. Dr. Pak continues to help me get things moving. I am grateful. The two nurses, Beauty and Jabara, still need direction. When I walked out to go to the bathroom, I was surrounded by a mob of girls, asking me my age, my name, telling me their names. This was a bright spot in my day. Director Chang caught this meeting on camera. We had a good evening devotion. Eun Jin expressed feelings of hopelessness that all the young girls want to do is get married. Then everyone got off in their solution to this. The director explained information about the culture here. Parents push marriage; in the Hindi culture, there is less money to give for the dowry if your daughter is younger. I found what he was saying interesting, but I am tired. I must need some quiet time.

We go on these trips and see the poverty and despair in the people, so we think we have the answer for them. We must always remember that God has the answers, and in his time, change will come; the people of Bangladesh must change their world. This whole process is long and sometimes painful. Connie shared how the people from church came to the Philippines and helped her as a child. She now gives back what was given to her.

February 8, 2011

We are on day three. Morning devotions were good. I believe the air and medications keep making me sick in the morning, but I will continue.

February 8,2011 1730

What a day! We started with devotions. David gave a devotions; he did a good job. He used a glass for explanation. Then we started with a boy [one of the school children] who had fallen and had an abrasion. Dr. Pak helped start IVs and I gave antibiotics. Right after I gave the antibiotic to this patient, she threw up a large amount. Her case had to be held till afternoon. We were able to recover and build up speed. We did four cases in the morning and four cases in the afternoon. I keep talking to the nurses; language is a problem but I try, and they help me learn their language. I try but it's hard.

After lunch we had a patient crying with her family. She did not want to undress. Beauty and I got her undressed. I had Sang check her. He said it was the worst case he had seen here, even worse than before. I could see in his eyes that he was trying to decide whether to do an operation or not. He said he will do her surgery. She is crying, not sure what to do. Then her brother comes in, asking if she had cancer or diabetes. I told him that we did not have the equipment to know if she had diabetes or cancer, but she has a severe prolapes. I told him that the doctor would come out and discuss whether they would operate. I put her and her brother in a room and told them that Dr. Lee would come out after he was done operating. They sat for a while as the staff explained this to the family. Finally I approached her to see if I could do her IV if she had surgery. She and her brother said yes; I started the IV and then Dr. Lee told the brother she was going to have the operation. We started antibiotics and away she went to surgery. This patient was the last case, so we were all tired.

She came to the recovery room with smiles. Her daughter was happy. Her brother was pleased. Dr. Lee explained all the restrictions and aftercare to her brother. The man was a Muslim and was rushing to a prayer meeting when Dr. Lee spoke with him. Sang asked if he wanted to pray with him; the man declined but later thanked Dr. Lee. The young nurse Beauty observed this surgery, so she saw the before and after difference. I was not as tired as I have been. We finished at 1700. Dinner was made by Toots. Evening devotions brought some sharing. Cathy was amazed at the work Sang does. Sang fell asleep after OR and missed dinner. He woke up at the end of devotions. Then the church members and he got talking about money. Cathy and I rounded without him. We had lots of complaints of pain, so Cathy ordered Tylenol 1000 mg. She told me to take extra, and sure enough, once one person got extra medication, they all wanted extra medication. The nurses were laughing, as we knew what was happening. Well, time for bed.

The ward after surgery

We would find out later that the brother was one of the leaders in the local mosque. We had no way of knowing this when the woman came. He would later tell Sang that he was pleased with the care his sister got. Thank you, God. I hope we changed how he viewed Christians and Americans. I can't imagine how hard it would be to trust people who look and speak different than you.

February 9, 2011

I forgot to write about one thing that Alex shared with us during evening devotions. He talked about two daughters of one of our patients. When he saw them enter the compound, they were veiled, but after they saw us and our care, they took off their veils. They spoke English and thanked us for helping their mother. They even asked Cathy for a picture with them. This was a highlight of her trip. Sometimes we don't see the whole picture, just our own world. The other thing that happened was when we were recovering our last patient. Beauty was so tired. There was a fly on the patient, so I was trying to explain to her what I was seeing; she did not understand me. So I started saying, "Buzz, buzz, buzz," with hand motion. She busted out laughing and laughing; the laugh was heard around the world between nurses after a long day. I felt I bonded with her. I have been trying to rest both nurses, as I'm sure they are new to this. Beauty and Jabara really want to work. I am trying to teach but still need to watch them. They both want to give medications, but I must watch the doses. After showing Jabara a few times, she was going to give 2 cc instead of 0.5 cc.

I now have to add Connie to my journal today. I had just finished writing when she asked if I was done journaling. I said, "Yes, but you are not in it." There was a bottle of water on the table. Connie said that it was hers. I insisted that it was mine, more than once. I told her that she must have left hers upstairs. I took a couple of sips and claimed the bottle as mine. When I went upstairs, I found my bottle! I met Connie on the stairs and told her, and then I asked her forgiveness and hugged her. We laughed, we laughed, we laughed. I can't believe I was so strong willed. Just a reminder of my weakness.

I am always learning something about myself. First, during this exchange I was loud, so everyone at breakfast heard this. I could not conceive that I could be wrong. Connie would say that just because I'm older doesn't mean I'm not forgetful. I even pointed out to her that I marked this bottle, therefore it was mine. I said this forcefully, with an attitude. Everyone was surprised that Connie backed down, but she was not going to fight with me, and I was not going to back down. I am humbled by the way I acted and need to remember this when I think that I'm right.

February 9,2011 2115

We did only four surgeries today. We went to Ulipur and had lunch with the kids. We were also presented to the class. [Rick helped present computers to the class and the teachers.] *Cathy spoke about the importance of staying in school. The director also dedicated a new worship center, and then he explained his plans for a gym. We had coffee in the Chilmary Medical Center house. We did one operation after lunch. I was so tired but it looked like we were going to finish early. Just as the last patient was leaving, people came in the building and said that there had been an accident. They brought in a man in acute pain, limping. I took him in the office and lay him down. I found myself surrounded by people who understood no English. I told someone to call for Dr. John. He came over, examined the man, and said he had a broken rib; we could give him Motrin for pain. The man was deaf and dumb. I asked John if I could give him Torodol. John said yes. We lay him down for a while, trying to decide how we would get him home. Rupal came and talked to him and helped him go home. I was scared but glad the outcome was good. Medical care is needed here. God, please help these people.*

What a busy day! Ulipur is the area that I wrote about years ago. Lepers who had been healed lived there with their families. There was also a school there, with about 200 children. The culture there is a mixture of Muslim and Hindi. The new worship center is for all faiths and was something that the local people wanted. It is important that we see the progress being made for the people. Once again we provided lunch for the children. It is so good to see all the children in school.

When I write about the last patient leaving, I mean being transferred to the room where their families and the local nurses take care of them. This area is still in the compound but not in the operating area. We were done with OR, so the doctors and Connie and Toots had gone back to our building to rest. I was the only medical person in that building when the people brought the man from the accident in. The man had been riding his bike and was hit by a motorcycle. The man who hit him was also there to see how he was. The injured man was holding his legs and had abrasions on his knees. I guess he was brought to us because we were there and the people knew we would help. I felt quite vulnerable as I was alone in the room. What made it harder was that I had no one who could translate. Lying the man down was the right thing to do. Then I called for John, who was still in the clinic across the way.

The man was in extreme pain, so when John suggested Motrin, I suggested Torodol, so he could get relief quicker. I was glad for my pediatrics experience; there was no way I could give him a shot in the buttocks, so I used his thigh. After about thirty minutes, we cleaned and bandaged his knees, and he was able to move. John said that he would be in a lot of pain for days. This experience made me realize that we need to get a hospital built here. My fear with this experience is once again not being good enough as a nurse to help, not knowing what to do. Also I am in a strange land and in a primitive setting with no language skills to understand the people's needs. The fact that this man was deaf and dumb was also a challenge.

February 10, 2011

I woke up early this morning with left leg pain, and then I took some Motrin. We are still laughing about the water bottle. I am always glad to provide entertainment. I am starting to miss home even though I like being here, even with the local people. I don't know if I wrote this but Mrs. Cushim said that her son wanted to study in America. She said that she had a friend in the States (meaning me).

To me, her statement was a great honor because I really love being with her. I also consider her my friend.

Kids eating in Ulipur, Bangladesh

February 10,2011 1900

We did five major operations and one incision and drainage today. We were slow and less confused than normal. The highlight of the day was when I heard the children drumming outside. I thought they were practicing. I saw some of the girls in beautiful, colorful red dresses. Then I heard noises in the gym from the kids. There was an assembly. I walked to the gym and saw 300 kids in white shirts sitting on the floor. They were being presented awards. I instantly started crying and couldn't stop. One of the local workers who was doing instruments and helped transport patients was standing there. He just kept looking at me. What a beautiful sight. The gym is large and white, with a large roof. I was not able to stay for two reasons; I would be getting a patient and I wanted Connie and Toots to see this sight.

Also I wanted Sang to see this. I went to the OR to push Connie out and tried to help Toots to get out. What a beautiful sight this was.

I was able to eat lunch. We only had one case after lunch. I started counting supplies and cleaning up. We finished by 1600. The director had awards with staff. We all sat in chairs outside. We all got to say something. The staff gave us letters of thanks. We got t-shirts along with the staff and took a group picture. I hugged Mrs. Cushim and called her my friend. I told her I would pray for her. I really love this woman and hope to keep in touch with her. In the evening, we had an Iron Chef contest between David and Rick, with no winners. David made ginger chicken soup. Rick made orange chicken stir fry. We were going to judge but had no time. We had devotions and debriefing (important). Most comments were good, except I brought up the problems we were having with orders for NPO (nothing by mouth). I also brought up the nurses' inexperience, but they were willing to work. Eun Jin said that she saw a difference in Chilmary and Ulipur.

The director went around the room and said something personal and positive about every one of us. He thanked Rick for the work with the computers and said how he was planning a computer school here. When he came to me, he made some profound statements. He said that many people in Bangladesh would remember me and talk about me, because with having surgery I was the first person they would see and last after surgery. He said that my touch would be remembered. I felt so humbled to think that I could make a difference.

We closed with a prayer. I rounded with Cathy; she wanted a patient catheterized. I had to go and find a catheter (she wanted a Foley). I walked out in the dark, went two places. When I got back, Cathy was leaving and wanted me to catheterize the patient. The last thing I wanted to do was catheterize a patient with little light, in the post-op area. I did it but only got 200 cc of clear urine. The patient was not drinking enough. Cathy said that at least we knew. Before dinner, Sang, Soo, Dr. Pak, and I were sorting through supplies. Sang was writing this information on a computer. He continued after debriefing and did not want help. We threw out loads of expired medications and had more room for new medications. Well, what a day. Good night. ☺

At the compound, we were guarded by military guards. We were told that the guards would volunteer for this assignment and considered this an honor. I remember while making rounds and checking on the women in the evening, the military guards would salute me when I walked past. They would click their heels and stand at attention. Understand that some people of Bangladesh did not consider women as equal. This was an honor and a very humbling experience for me. I never felt that I deserved such an honor, but this action showed me the heart of the people of Bangladesh.

February 11, 2011

I remember that it's Barbara's birthday. I really miss her. We are going home. It's 0530 and we are awake and ready to go. The power was on for a few minutes, and then the power was out, so I showered with my little flashlight. Rick showered by candlelight. I am wearing my scrubs till after rounds. I don't want any accidents on my clothes. I am worried about the trip home. I hate the ride. I will do a lot of praying. Alyssa has called Rick seven times, and we are worried.

February 11,2011 0750

Update: as we were praying for Alyssa, she sent Rick a text, saying that it could wait till Sunday. Our last devotion was short and to the point; it takes time to process what we went through. We did morning rounds. All our patients seem to be doing well. Most of them still complain of pain. The local nurses are eager and have learned how to take out a Foley. I am flattered that they do it the same way as I did it. [Because of how the beds and room was set up, without a bathroom and sink, I would squirt the saline from the balloon against the wall, and that is what the local nurses did.]

February 11,2011 0840

We are on the bus going back home. The bus was late so we went to meet the bus; everyone was looking at us at the bus stop.

As we are standing on top of Madame Chang's home, getting ready to leave, the director is giving us last minute instructions through Alex (the director speaks Korean). This will be our first ride home since the accident. The director tells us how he did some research on accidents when groups do medical work overseas and said that most accidents occur on the trip out of the country. Thanks for this information. That was not what I needed to hear. I found that what he said stirred up much fear inside me. I was so glad that we started praying because I felt my fear going away. I have come a long way from the first trip I made to Bangladesh. I also have a deeper faith and a better relationship with God.

February 12, 2011

Well, in three hours we will be on our second leg of the trip. Let me backtrack on what happened on February 11. The bus ride is so long. The drive was going fast through towns and making wonderful time. We stopped halfway for lunch at that nice Chinese restaurant. I kept listening to my music. Rick just kept looking outside for hour after hour. As a group, we didn't talk much. I went to the bathroom, squatting again, hard to do with pants. I have to take my one leg out or I will wet my clothes; hard to do in an outhouse. We got to Dhaka just when the factories were letting out from work, even though it was Sunday. Dhaka smells bad. I see at least fifteen smoke stacks off in the distance.

February 13, 2011

I was too tired to finish last night. We now are at the airport, awaiting the flight home. We woke up at 0230, took a taxi, and went through customs fast here [Singapore]. To continue from yesterday: The traffic is bad [Bangladesh], and the director wants us to go to a Korean restaurant. It was 1830 and we had a 2230 flight. Rick is irritable. He just wanted to go to the airport. He doesn't want to miss our flight. He can't understand why we are doing this. He is restless. I have tried to calm him down, but it's not working. He is irritable with me. We got to the Korean restaurant, and

Connie met two workers stationed in Dhaka. These workers kept Connie company while she stayed there. The director wanted them to see each other again. I chose not to sit with Rick. We ate wonderful Korean food, fast. I stop worrying. We got to the airport in time but so much confusion. Everyone took the bags, but I kept looking for mine and cannot find it. I kept saying that maybe it's on the bus and I am going without it. Rick (who is already irritable) becomes more irritable. Finally we discover my bag; what a relief. I just feel better knowing it's with me. The check-in is not easy. The people can't understand that we are checking our bags (the bags that we brought supplies in) all the way to Detroit, and because it's two different airlines, they are having a hard time processing the bags. They had to call their supervisor for this. Finally, we go through.

Next step, going through immigration. Here is where we have a problem. The line for foreigners is clearly marked. All of a sudden, this Bangladesh man, dressed in a suit, cuts in front of me. I say no, that I was there first. He comes back with a supervisor; he is pushing his weight around. I go through; Soo told me later that this same man tried this again with her, and she said no. This is not right. After that we go through security for the flight, long lines. You have to be patted down in a secure room with a woman. The mosquitoes are as bad all over, and then we board.

We are on the plane. Suddenly, Rick is relaxed. He's a totally different person. I am so tired. When we get to Singapore, it will be 0530 because of the time change. This is only a four-hour flight. How do you process an eight-hour bus ride through Bangladesh? How do you process seeing poverty, skinny women, no machines to do farming, poor roads, tin roofs, dirt roads, bikes carrying heavy loads, busses, cars, oxen, people carrying baskets on their heads, all on a two-lane road (not like a road we think of)? They drive the British way (on the wrong side of the road). There are high hills on the side with a drop; we come to speed bumps in every town. Every bus has scrapes and many broken windows. I still cannot get over how many people ride on the top of the bus. I can't imagine doing this, and I am sure people die. Because of the floods, there is no burial in Bangladesh, only cremation. This time on the bus, we were higher up, so we had a different perspective. On the bus we see a few businesses open in some of the towns.

[It was a holiday, so many business were closed.] We pass an area with lots of bananas, and to our eyes, it looks like there is lots of food, but there are a lot of people in Bangladesh, people without money. People with handicaps like the man who was deaf and dumb and was hit by the motorcycle. This time I saw another woman without an eye (no artificial eye for her). Even when I go back I must remember that I am an eyewitness to these things. I can't forget these people.

My feelings for the woman without an eye are strong, as my best friend Sharon has one eye. She had her eye removed when she was two years old. We have been friends since we were twelve years old. We went to the same grade school and worked together at the bank. Sharon stood up in my wedding. We have traveled together and had children at the same time. Sharon is someone who has stood with me through thick and thin. She is one of the first persons I call when things are good and bad. I have great love and affection for her. She will be helping me edit this book. I have admired that Sharon does not let her vision stop her. She became a social worker in spite of the difficulty going to school with limited vision. Sure, there are times that she chose not to do something because she might get hurt, but if it's possible, she is right there.

One example of this is when we went to Haleakala in Maui. We stopped at a roadside lookout at about 7,000 feet elevation, high about the clouds, and Sharon got her hiking stick out and walked the path on this mountain with Al, so she could experience the feel of the mountain. I will never forget looking on that mountain and seeing her standing there, taking it in. When I am in Bangladesh and see how the woman without the eye is treated, I think of Sharon. I want the possibilities my friend Sharon has had, I want an artificial eye for this woman. I have seen the possibilities this woman has. I can't forget these people.

We arrived in Singapore at 0500 am and good news: three rooms were ready. One for girls, one for guys, and then they gave Rick and me our own room. A room with a king size bed. Even though I slept about three hours on the plane, I am exhausted. We made plans to meet at 0900.

am The bed is so soft, the sheets are soft and clean. I can't believe how good this feels. I feel spoiled, blessed. I know I should feel guilty because of what I have just seen, but not today. Thank you, God. We get a call at 0910: "Where are you?" We overslept. We both shower and met up with everyone.

We go to a small mom and pop restaurant in Singapore. I had French toast with coconut jam, really good. Then off to shopping but first find an ATM. It's hot in Singapore, bright sun. we walk through some malls. We split up; sixteen people is too hard to keep going. Some go back to the hotel and rest. We go to Lucky Plaza Asian Mall. We can barter here. We buy T-shirts, a kimono, bags, cheap; with the exchange rate and bartering, we do good. I also bought a jade necklace. I went to a store and saw deep green jade stones but pricey $200 (Singapore). The lady added four extra beads, a better clasp, and four strands (to hold the beads together) for me to wear. It looks good on me. I wore it yesterday all day. Cathy had a suit and dress made. She also bought a tablecloth and then found someone who would have charged her less.

When I was buying the jade I asked for Connie and Chong-Hui's input; both felt I was paying too much. Because of this, the lady was sweeter, thus giving me the extra beads. We went to a local restaurant for my birthday, all twenty-one of us. David's wife is from Singapore so she picked the restaurant, and she and David helped us order. The food was so good: chicken, soup, noodles, fish, rice, pork, lime drinks. They sang "Happy Birthday" and thanked us [Rick and I paid for the dinner]. I was glad Julie was there to help.

We took a cab to the new Shy Marina; what a building! Three towers with what looks like a ship on it. We went up to the top, all fifty-six floors. There was a large observation deck. It was so beautiful, seeing all around. You could see that Singapore was an island. They built a swimming pool up there. We were able to see the pool but not use it; it was for hotel guests only. The pool cascaded down. The spa looks like it is at the edge. This is really beautiful and breath-taking. We then go to the casino. Rick plays and loses a few dollars. Mr. Kim, Chong-Hui, and Cathy are there with us. I sit and watch Rick play. After we are done, we go walking the mall and find a boat ride. The casino is in a very high end mall, so I don't buy anything. We get free water in the casino, but I don't know if they give drinks. The charge to get in is free for foreigners but there is a charge for local people. There is no place to sit down so we do a lot of walking.

Connie had a hard time and needed to be driven to the restaurant. We ate dinner at a dim sum restaurant, good food, very good. Then we walked back to the hotel for devotions. Our last night together. We meet in our room because it was a big room. David led devotions. There was quietness. You could tell we were tired but we needed to process the last day. We prayed, talked, and said good-bye to Alex, Serena, and the kids. Alex and David wanted to see us off, but we told them not to get up so early. We slept for a few hours and flew to Tokyo. The connecting flight was quick so we went up to the Delta lounge for only a few minutes and then got back on the plane again. No TV, and we are in the back, so it's hard to see the monitor.

We still have four hours to go on the flight, but I have some final thoughts. I know that the daily diary, because of my exhaustion, does not tell the total picture of what I experience; how could it? I would have to write all day long for you to understand. I am so grateful to God for allowing me this experience. But because of my trips, I have uncovered many of my fears, and most days I am content. I have a purpose. We all know the task before us is overwhelming. I don't know why God in this time and place wants change. Because of Christ's death, change has already occurred. I don't know it all, but I know we must continue to work to help the people of Bangladesh. I don't know if I will go back. If God calls me, I will. I have friends there, and I love being with them.

Connie is using a wheelchair in the airport. Sang said that she was moving slower, so I think her purpose was to show God's goodness. Cathy will be going to Africa in April. If I had to bet, I believe Toots is done too. Alex will work from Singapore. Eun Jin feels urgency and is a tireless worker. John, I believe, will continue this work. Mr. Kim is happy when he is there; he has a sense of purpose. Chong-Hui will work again. Gu (Mr. Nine) will come back as his business allows. Soo and Sang will continue because both have a heart for this work. Dr. Pak will work as long as he has health. These are the people I have grown to love, and they add color and joy to my life. They are my brothers and sisters in Christ. I am so blessed and humbled to know them. Thank you, Jesus.

February 16, 2011

We have been home for a few days. We came home on Sunday; my feet felt tight in the airport. My pants felt tight. When I came home and looked at my feet, they were so swollen. I have never seen them so swollen, my legs also. I could barely walk. I put my feet up at 1800 and was falling asleep. Finally at 1900 my family told me to go to bed. I slept till 0430. That felt so good. Gina, Gibson, and Alyssa were here. Alyssa made lemon chicken. What a sweet thing to do. Monday and Tuesday, I was feeling weak and thought it was jet lag. Today I woke up with a headache and cough. I went to see Dr. Geimer; I have a sinus infection. She increased my Dixcocillin and gave me nasal spray and an inhaler. I have been resting most of the day.

After we came back from Bangladesh, I feel I was told to write the story, so I wrote all of the above. As I was doing that, new thoughts would come to me, and I would hear that I should include the following thoughts. I know that they may seem out of place, but I am including them. I hope that you can follow my thoughts. Some of these thoughts are about Bangladesh, some are the thoughts of an old nurse.

Art Contest in Bangladesh

One of the things Eun Jin works on is having the classes draw pictures, and we have an art contest. The children can use all kinds of supplies; we bring color pencils, crayons, markers, and paper. Eun Jin gives a topic to reflect on, but we are aware that we must respect the Muslim culture and not make the topic too spiritual. Eun Jin collects the drawings by classes, and then in our evening time, she asks us to be the judges for the contest. She arranges prizes for the winners. Judging these drawings is hard. We all have our opinion of art. What I like, you may not like, so we sometimes have to go by what the majority feels is the best. What I have noticed when we see the drawings is the pride these children have for their country, Bangladesh. I know that we have pride in our country, but because of the poverty I see in Bangladesh, I guess I never thought that the people would have pride for where they live. I see in many of the drawings the flag of Bangladesh.

I see the town square not far from where we are. I see the boats and the river down the road from where we are. I see the farms and the houses where the children live. I also see the mosques. The drawings have helped me see more clearly from the children's eyes what life is like for them. These drawings have showed me that we are connected as people of the same human family. Art does show us the human story. The winners of the contest get recognition and a prize and show pride for a job well done.

Morning in Bangladesh

One of the things I like in Bangladesh is the morning devotions with the workers of Chilmary Medical Center. We enter the room and remove our shoes, so you can imagine how many shoes are down at the bottom of the stairs. We sit in chairs and the music starts. We sing hymns. Here we are, all singing in our native languages. The instruments are some type of organ and a tambourine. We sing for a while, and then someone reads from the Bible, and then one of us gives our testimony. Then the staff goes on to tell the events of the day and what each person's role is. I can feel the presence of God in these early morning devotions. I always feel so blessed to be sharing this moment in time with the people of Bangladesh and my friends.

After we are done, we go outside (after the scramble to get our shoes back on). Then we line up and begin the morning exercise. The exercises are done to commands from a recording and involve every muscle group. This is quite fun, and we always join in. Then the anthem and pledge of Bangladesh is said, along with a chant that ends with a joyous shout: "Yay!" Then the children turn and face us and say, "Good morning," and ask us how we are doing. I love this part because you can see the children's faces and the happiness they have. Then the children march passed us and greet us individually. Here is where my heart melts, and I know why I am here and why I keep coming back. Here is when I learn to love people who live in a country so different from mine. Here is when I know God loves all the people of the world. How blessed am I to be able to share this time and space with God's family.

Nurses and Doctors

Saying "nurses and doctors" sounds weird. It's usually said "doctors and nurses," but since I am a nurse, I chose it to be this way for today. I could have titled this "My Journey with Doctors," but I stick with my title. I was twenty-two when I started working in the hospital with doctors. I was just a young, naïve women growing up in middle class America. I was shy, especially around men. Most of the doctors I first came in contact with were men, though as a teenager, I had gone to a woman doctor. The doctors I remember from the early years include Dr. Dethi, an Indian, and the first Indian I had come in contact with. Dr. Dethi was a kind and gentle man, and I respected him so much that my husband would see him. Later in my career, I would work with his daughter, who became a family practice doctor. The world sometimes is smaller than we think.

Two doctors I remember because of the times were Dr. Vine, OB/GYN, and Dr. Antess, a pediatrician; both of these doctors were African Americans. Both were young doctors with wit and personality. Both commanded respect and were well liked by staff. The year I graduated was 1972 and I stayed at this hospital for three years. The reason I explain this was that the riots in Detroit were in 1967. This means that both of these doctors were probably going to medical school during the riots.

Doctors at this small hospital were treated much like doctors at the time were. The nurses would round with doctors; what the doctors said went. Doctors were above the nurses, and I was scared of doctors. My insecurities would come out when I was around doctors. I tried to do everything right and not cause anyone to notice me. I knew that you didn't want to get a doctor mad at you, because that would cause trouble. I worked like this for three years. When I came back from having my daughter, I was pulled to post partum when a nurse had a day off; I never dreamed in those days that I would finish my nursing career on post partum.

The job at Children's would be an eye opener as far as my relationship with the doctors. We would work with residents, fellows, and department heads. Suddenly I was working with residents and calling them by their first names. This was new for me and seemed foreign. In July, the new residents started, so they would ask me for help, I find myself having to tell them what to do. I see their stress and that they are human. We are a team, we talk to each other, nurses are included in rounds, and after all, we know the babies better. I am even asked my opinion. I start feeling better about myself as I realize that we are all learning and the good of the patient is what counts. I feel that those six years I really grow as a nurse; I was challenged but learned so much.

I learned that doctors work long hours, that their training is brutal, and that I never had any desire to be a doctor. I would not like being on call for thirty-six hours, trying to stay awake and give the best care to my patient. I have seen doctors staying up all night and at 0600 nodding out on charts as they are trying to put in orders only to have to rounds by 0800, doing all this with no sleep. I know that most doctors do not go through this for the money, but they have a gift that they share with us. While at Children's I starting to see women becoming doctors, and I could see the sacrifice that they make. I met a fellow whose parents are taking care of her son because of the hours she kept at work. I met highly motivated and intellect people training to take care of patients. I also met jerks who give us nurses a hard time. Usually this occurred off shift when you are trying to get orders and give reports and patient conditions. I am less intimidated by them, because the good of the patient matters to me. Fortunately, there are fewer jerks than ones who care not only about their patients but about me, teaching me and helping me grow. Some of the department heads I worked with still work there and are the cutting edge of new treatments at Children's.

My job at Beaumont would bring me some new experience with doctors again. I was the midnight nurse in pediatrics with no doctors to cover except the house doctor, who was an internist. I was alone, therefore I would notify the on call doctors in the middle of night if I felt anything was wrong or if I needed orders. Calling the on call doctor would present some issues, as they did not know these children. If the patients came from emergency room, I had orders from the emergency doctor (which was good). I wouldn't see the doctors except those who would round early. Dr. Blank was one of then, again a very nice Indian doctor. I learned to do a lot of thinking on my own, as what I needed to call for and what could wait.

One of the staff doctors would go to my boss every time I called (which was rare) and complain that I called. He would send his patients to Royal Oak Beaumont because he didn't want to be called at night and Royal Oak had night coverage. I would tell my boss that I called so she knew what he would complain about before he found her. I found myself going back in time as I had come from a place of being part of a team to seeing doctors as adversaries. I was the only nurse with a nursing assistant and secretary, so I had no one to bounce ideas off.

One of my experiences of being yelled at by a doctor occurred at this time. I arrived at 2300 with a report that we had a nine-year-old coming as a direct admit from Bad Axe, Michigan. He had jumped feet first into a pond. He was coming by ambulance. He arrived about 2345, so the afternoon shift had left. When I examined him, I observed that he could not move his legs and urine was dripping from his penis (not a good sign). I was quite upset and concerned for this patient and called his private doctor with what I observed. He wanted a consult with a neurosurgeon tonight.

Here is where I made my mistake. I asked him if I should call, and of course he said yes, and I made that call. The neurosurgeon proceeded to yell at me, tell me it was too late for him to see this child. He later came in to see the child and was nicer to me. He was mad that the private doctor had not called him early in the evening to tell him that this child was coming so he could have rested, since he had early surgery. I learned my lesson about not getting in the middle of what should be a doctor-to-doctor discussion. The neurosurgeon would later take care of my mother and was totally different to me as a family member.

When I left pediatrics to go to OB, once again my relationship with doctors changed. I started working with more female doctors, both in special care nursery and post partum. I have gotten to know some wonderful doctors. I feel that we have a good relationship. We get to know them and they get to know us. Where I feel we have really got to know each other better is in the circumcision room. When you are doing a circumcision with a doctor, there is time for talking, asking how things are going, how's the family, and sharing thoughts. I have had some interesting conversations over a circumcision and have heard some conversations between doctors that involved their practice that maybe I should not have heard. I have a slogan: "What's said in the circ room stays in the circ room."

Sometimes we nurses can give doctors a hard time. For example, one day a doctor came to me and asked me nicely to do circumcision with him. It was a busy day and I said no, but I was only joking. The next thing I knew, he was gone. I felt that maybe one too many nurses had given him a rough time that day and he didn't want to deal with one more nurse. I felt bad about this. I heard later from my boss that we could not refuse to do a circumcision. I knew I had to make amends and say I was sorry. The next time we were alone, I told him I was sorry. To this day we have a good relationship.

Building good relationships is hard and just like any relationship, it takes time. Nurses look out for doctors more than most doctors would like to admit. We know the patients and are a go-between from patient and doctor. For example, a doctor did not discharge a patient, so I called the on call doctor because the patient was anxious to go home. The doctor discharged the patient over the phone. Because no doctor had seen the patient, I asked the doctor if she would talk with the patient, and she said, "I guess that's important to you." I ignored the comment and handed the phone to the patient. The patient left feeling that her doctor cared, rather than her doctor was too busy for her. This is what nurses do: think about the patient.

Doctors are intelligent people who train hard, work long hours, and really don't get paid as much as they should. I don't begrudge what they have. I didn't want to be a doctor. I don't think I have what it takes. I would not want to hold people's lives in my hands; this is what surgeons do. I would not want to have everything I owned in my spouse's name because I could be sued for everything I possess. Some of my doctor friends pay at least $100,000 in liability insurance in case of being sued. Most of my doctor friends have had someone try to take them to court for damages; all this for trying to help people. As a nurse, I can receive some of these issues but not near as much as a physician. I am happy being a nurse. I never in my wildest dreams thought I would interact socially with doctors: going out to eat with doctors, going to their homes, traveling with them. All in all, I am a nurse who is glad to be in a profession where I have met some wonderful doctors.

Changes, Changes, Changes

After thirty-nine years as a nurse, here are some of the changes I have seen:

Diabetics would have their insulin given according to sugar and acetone in the urine, versus one touch machines with instant blood sugar readings.

Expanding of the *Physician's Desk Reference* versus looking up drugs on computer.

White uniforms versus colored uniforms (and in some hospitals, prints).

Hats (nursing caps) versus no hats (wearing a hat could be fun, especially if your hat got caught on the curtain or IV pole).

Not wearing gloves (you might offend a patient if you did not wear gloves) versus wearing gloves to give care.

Cranked beds versus electric beds.

TV on wheels shared between patients versus everyone gets a TV, even in the emergency room.

Sippy diets (milk and Maalox) for ulcers versus medications for ulcer treatment.

Restraints (Posey, arm restraints, leg restraints) versus sitters (people assigned to sit with patient) versus TV monitors to watch patients.

Being hospitalized the night before for x-ray and surgical procedures.

Having more managers than staff on duty.

No more eight-hour shifts, twelve-hour shifts only.

No more forty or thirty-six hours per week, several thousand dollars less a year.

Overtime only for a forty-hour week; working sixteen-hour shifts does not count as overtime.

Pay cuts.

Being sent home if there are no patients versus the hospital keeping its commitment to staff.

Walking reports or report in front of the patient or standing outside of the patient's room; this might mean waking the patient up in the morning to introduce the new nurse.

Mandatory in-services on computer (these may be done at home on your own time).

Shared governing versus managers guiding the unit.

Hard to get your vacation; the unit only allows so many vacations, and there is no one to cover.

Combined Time Off versus vacation days.

Scripts for what we should say to the patients versus I get to choose how I will speak with my patients.

Room service (meaning the patient can choose what they want to eat and when they want to eat).

Nursing assistants taking out Foley catheters versus only nurses can remove them.

Phonies (meaning I am available at all times including when I go to the bathroom and at lunch).

Writing my name on a chalk board versus what is a chalk board?

Machines for everything: IVAC machines for IV versus using your eyes for regulating the flow of the IV.

Machines for taking temperature versus glass thermometers.

Machines for taking blood pressures versus blood pressure spothemeters.

Public sitz bath versus my own sitz bath.

Semiprivate rooms (and sometimes wards) after giving birth versus private rooms where the dad can spend the night.

Father not in delivery rooms versus anyone the mother wants can be in the delivery room.

All babies went to the nursery for eight hours after delivery versus the mother can hold and feed her baby right after birth.

First feeding the baby got was water by bottle versus infant goes to breast right after delivery.

Breast-feed infant was given water after feeding versus infant given breast milk only.

Parents not seeing infant and children getting blood taken and IV starts away from parents.

Patients had a menu to choose from versus I can call for food anytime I want.

Doctor standing and talking to their patients versus doctors sitting and talking to their patients.

Not all of these changes have been bad. The patients love the chance to choose their own food, and patients love that they know their nurses. The care of diabetics is much better with the one touch. I liked the machines after I learned how to use then. Some of the changes have been hard to deal with; the loss of income has been hard. The working hard and giving good care all morning without breakfast or lunch, only to be told you must go home now and must use your CTO time or EA, which means you do not get paid but it is not counted against you.

The hardest for me has been the computer for nursing. When I was in high school, I took typing and hated it. I knew I'd never use typing, I was going to be a nurse. Fast forward thirty-nine years, I use my typing skills every day at work. I am grateful that I took typing. The problem with the computers is just when we learn what they want us to chart, they change the program. On our unit, the computer from labor does not "talk" to the computer on post partum, so we have to put the information in the computer again. (Since I wrote this, they have changed this, I'm sure at a large cost.)

Also, we are doing more charting than we did before, so this takes more time and takes us away from the patient and their care. This is my second time learning how to use computers as a nurse, and some systems are more user friendly than others. Also, in the system we are using now, there are many ways to chart the same thing, so I can do it one way and my friend can do it another way. I also feel that we are learning the system with staff helping and that education is being cut all the time, so I'm never sure if I am doing what they want me to chart the right way. Whether I like it or not, computers in nursing are here to stay, so I try to do the best I can. The things I like about computers is that I can be in a patient's room and look up something about that patient or another patient without going to the desk. The information is available as soon as possible.

Who, Me Teach?

I never wanted to be a teacher. The thought of being in a classroom with thirty children never was something I wanted to do, nor did I think I would be good at teaching. When I started nursing, I was like a sponge, taking everything in, learning all the time. Then the years went by, and I learned so much that I found myself teaching. What I can tell you about nursing is that we do so much teaching. We teach our patients all the time. We translate what their doctors say, so that the patient can understand what is going on in their bodies. We explain many times what they are going through. We prepare them and their families for the care they will need at home; an example of this is teaching diabetic patients how to give themselves insulin shots.

I find now that I love teaching and am fairly good as a teacher (at least that's what the students and my patients tell me). At my age now, I find myself drawn to the students. I don't know if it's because it hasn't always been an easy journey for me or because I want there to be good nurses, because someday they will be taking care of me or my family; whatever it is, I do take time with the students. My educational background does not allow me to be an instructor, but I have had several students tell me I would be good at that. I'm not sure about that, as the thought of watching seven or eight students would be hard. I quiz the students; I ask them why we are doing this and what they are assessing; I ask if it is normal. Sometimes I feel like I intimidating the student, but I tell them I am not their instructor and I don't grade them; I am just getting them to think. Most of the students like this and like the fact I am interested in them. I have taken a senior student for a whole semester and find this rewarding, because we have time to work through some things.

The other part of teaching as a nurse involves the patient. Because I now work the mother–baby unit, I teach all the time. I love teaching parents how to give their infant a bath. I am known to involve the fathers and even siblings in the first bath. If the dad wants, I have him help me give the first bath to the newborn. Most dads love this and thank me for the experience. I also became a lactation consultant and teach parents about breast-feeding all the time. I believe this is the best way for infants to be fed, so this teaching can be difficult at times. Many women lack confidence, so I involve the fathers and family when I can. I find I can be a passionate teacher in what I believe, so I have learned to be an educator and let the parents make their own decisions. This approach works better for them and me.

I also teach the new moms about themselves. I love doing discharge teaching. This is a time I remember as a new mom. I was a nurse when my daughter was born, but I did not work OB and really didn't know what I was doing. I always try to remember my feelings, so I spend much time with the family. I don't just hand papers to them and say good-bye. I believe we give so much paperwork and the parents don't have time to go through all of it, so I review the paperwork with them. I encourage them to ask questions. I like both parents to be present, so what one doesn't hear the other does, but I don't really want the siblings present, as children have a short attention span, and the child's life has been changed by the birth of this child already, which means they may be acting out while I am talking.

My passion about this teaching has brought me many rewards, and parents remember me and are glad to have me as a nurse. The other place I have taught is when I am on my trips overseas. In the Philippines, I was often surrounded by nursing students. I had to teach them sterile technique, otherwise they would have contaminated the surgical field. In Bangladesh, I was teaching all the time, though language was a problem. I am a fairly patient person so I guess teaching is a good thing for me.

Korean Methodist Church

The first time I walk into the Korean church, I was a little confused. All I saw were Korean people; some spoke English, some spoke broken English. I was handed a translator, and the person looked for Dr. Lee. They somehow knew I wasn't quite sure where I belonged. Going into that church opened up a whole new world to me. First of all, it was the first time I was someplace where I had to use a translator. The service was pretty similar to what I knew from the Catholic church. The structure of the service was similar. This was good for me, so I could follow. The church was packed with people, and everyone was singing. People didn't look at me, and I felt at home. I was greeted by people, and they bowed to me. The choir was great, and I found myself crying. I couldn't believe that God had taken me here. To hear people worshiping God in different languages was beyond words that I can describe.

Before we go to Bangladesh, we are presented to the church for a blessing. Our names are called out loud, and the church prays over us. The team leader is presented with certifications for all of us. He will hand these to us later. While we are presented to the church, I can feel the special blessing, and this last time, I could feel the Holy Spirit sending us out to Bangladesh. What a blessing to be part of this church, and I feel I am a part of this church. I have been blessed to have many meals and attended many services at this church. I will always be grateful to this church for allowing me to go on several trips with them.

CHAPTER 10:

Contiuning the journey.

January 17, 2012

Well, I'm on the plane headed for Bangladesh. This is my fifth trip there, and I'm happy to be going back on this adventure. I'm excited to be going with my friends and seeing my other friends. We have been preparing for weeks. There are fifteen of us from the Korean Methodist church and seven from the Korean Presbyterian church. Fifteen of us are on the plane now. Eun Jin and John Lee are flying a different way, through Dubai, and will be there before us. We will have a little more down time in Singapore again. On Sunday, the KMC sent us off. We went in front of the church again. We took Sharon Lotoczky to church with us because she loves music and because she knows the story. She really enjoyed the service. As I was standing in front of the church, with them praying over us, I felt the spirit come into me. I really can't believe this is my fifth trip. What a blessing. One of the blessings before the trip was a joint communion service between KMC and KPC. We received communion: bread and wine. The pastor from KMC officiated. I had to work so I was late. We went around the room, explaining why we were going. I didn't get to hear anyone else but I did make the service. I was glad and grateful. Here are the people going with me:

Dr. Choon Pak: team leader. From what I have heard, this will be his last trip. I really love being with him. Dr. Pak is a gentle and thoughtful man. He has a quiet spirit about him.

Dr. Sang Lee: the reason I'm going. I worry about him, as he is the only surgeon. He works much too hard and has been up late all week with operations and delivering a baby.

Eun Soo Lee: I think of her as my sister in Christ. I always enjoy her company. She takes care of the money.

Celia Mateo (Toots): one of the warmest, most giving people I know. Toots runs a tight OR.

Connie Escrupolo: she's going back! Her faith is unshaken. She loves the Lord and will do what he asked. She had a shoulder operation this year from chasing after her great-nephew.

Sara Seung Chung: she is a young Korean with a joyful heart. I can't wait to get to know her better.

Mr. Kyu Yang: he will be our soccer coach. He is a tall Korean man that I hope to get to know better.

Mr. Kim: our team leader last year. He lives in Texas now so it is great to be with him.

Gu Jae Kwon (Mr. Nine): he's back. He is quiet, a joyful man, and it's great being with him.

Song: the man from my first trip. I saw his wife Soo again. It's always great to see them. I remember that he cried in Bangladesh and his heart is there, so I'm glad he is coming.

Frank Manalisay: he is from Guam and doesn't speak Korean. He is worldly and intelligent and eager to help.

Mi Kyong Manalisay: Frank's wife. She is Korean and a joy to be around. We are already bonding, as his daughter had a son when she was eighteen years old.

Mr. Young Kim: I don't know him well. He is Korean and smiles a lot.

The rest of the team is coming from a different direction:

Dr. John Lee: I love John. I see him at the gym all the time. He is intelligent and caring and fun to be with.

Dr. Hong: I just met him so I'm not sure. He seems so intellectual.

Director David: up to the last minute, he didn't know if he was coming, but I heard he got his passport and will be joining us.

Eun Jin Lee: she is my sister in the Lord also. Her father has cancer and her sister is in California to help him. I can't imagine what stress she is under. I'm glad she is coming. She begged the director for her group to come.

John: I forgot to include him in my diary. He is a lawyer who had been to Bangladesh before. I don't know him well.

We are picking up two people in Singapore:

Serena Kim: Alex's wife. She will be helping us with nursing. This is a treat for me as maybe I will have someone to help me.

Christa: she is a grant writer. She will try to write a grant to fund the hospital in Chilmary. When I started this journey, there was no hospital. I now know that we might actually build a hospital. I continue to write because I have been told that my writing will help this.

We had a busy year this year, six parties at our house:

Sharon Lotoczky: sixty years old, given by her children, no food preparation, just clean up.

Susan Todd: graduation party, given by her children, clean up and set up.

My nephew's graduation: clean up and set up.

Father's Day: Food, clean up, and set up.

Mark's going away: Food, clean up, and set up.

Ray's funeral: My cousin Ray, who was my cousin Barbara's common-law husband, died of a heart attack in his bed. His son Jessie found him. So in two years, Jessie and his brother lost both of their parents. Needless to say it's been hard on them. Ray told the boys he did not want a funeral but wanted a party, so we volunteered our house. He was cremated, so a week later we did a memorial service. We ordered Polish food from Lukich, and Pastor David from Zion came and did a service. The boys were grateful, and Ray's sister and brother were pleased. Jessie gave us $300, which went to Bangladesh. We also did two dinners to fund raise for Bangladesh, totaling $1,600.

This year I feel a change in the people where I work. Prudi Manzella and Michelle handed me money before I left. This money went to Madame Yoo's computer mouse. One of the things the nurses' council did was to have a bake sale to raise money. They raised $1,700; the sale was headed by Nancy Herman. Dr. Lee and I did a poster board. I think this helped people to see what we do. It was humbling for me when people asked me about it. I always want them to know that I never intended to take any money from them. Any money they give me goes for Bangladesh. After seeing what I have seen, how could I take money? There has to be some sacrifices in what we do.

One of the things that happened this year was that Mark moved in September. He got a job offer in Florida. It was a good offer so he packed up his truck and moved. It's been lonely without him. It was hard to see him go. He came for Christmas and enjoyed himself. He was following Rick and myself around, just talking our ears off. By the way, I didn't mention that Rick also on the plane. He's doing computers again. This is his third trip, and it's a blessing that he is with us.

Mark's daughter Alyssa turned sixteen years old this year. Now she has a boyfriend and I'm worried. All I can do is talk. Alyssa's mom had a daughter this year, so I hope that helps Alyssa remember her goals. Brittany (Gina's stepdaughter) is also sixteen and has a boyfriend. So I have promised both of them a trip on graduation to Rome. I for one can't wait to go to Rome.

One of the happiest things that happened this year was the birth of Barbara Ann Frieda Holden, my granddaughter. What a joy. She was named after my cousin Barbara. I think this was a wonderful choice, as Barbara was Gina's godmother. The birth of this granddaughter was special. I think of the girls born all over the world, and I'm so grateful Barbara was born here in the United States. I once heard Beth Moore talk about the birth of her granddaughter and what it means, because in some parts of the world, girls are sold into slavery or prostitution. Why is that with all the improvements in the world, we still look at women as sex objects? I'm so upset with the videos and how the young women are selling their bodies. I watched "New Year's Eve Rock and Roll" and was upset with how they dressed. I guess sex sells, and we really have not changed since ancient times when we worshipped Baal (the sex god).

Barbara has brown hair and a great smile. Our grandson Gibson is so cute and smart. Rick is watching the children in the mornings, and I am watching then at least once a week. We love the children but it is not easy. I have to remember that my mother helped us out. I just wish it was easier for Rich and Gina.

We are still doing Bible study. We are studying John this year. I'm enjoying this study so much. Two things that the study of John said: in John 5:6, when Jesus asked the blind man, "Do you want to get well?" what a profound statement. Jesus wasn't just talking about physically well but spiritually well also. Since reading that, whenever I go back to my negative thinking, I ask myself, "Do I want to get well? Do I want the joy only Jesus can give me?" I need to stay grounded and keep in touch with Jesus. Another sermon I heard at the church was "Remember Jesus Christ"; this helps when I am troubled and feel I can't go on. When I feel I can't work another minute with the pressures and constant changes, I need to "Remember Jesus Christ," and he will guide my steps and give me strength to do his will; all I need to do is ask.

January 19, 2012

We always lose a day in travel. I'm in the Singapore Airport waiting for the flight. It's about 1530, and we don't even know what gate our flight is at. We stayed in the transit hotel. The flight from Tokyo was long; I was tired and didn't stay awake for the food. I woke up feeling very sick, like I was going to throw up. I got some ginger ale from the flight attendant and felt better. We were in the exit seat, with three of us in a row. We didn't look back; there lots of empty seats, and we could have had a row to ourselves. We got to Singapore and found the hotel at the airport, room rented by the hour. We stayed six hours, from 0100 to 0700. The room was clean, not like the last time we stayed in the hourly hotel after our accident. Rick and I slept. It felt so good to put my legs up, as both of my legs are starting to swell.

We got up at 0615 and showered. It always feels so good after a long trip to shower. We met for breakfast in the food court, each of us having our own choices. Rick and I have eggs, toast, half a banana. The rest of the group has noodles and rice. After breakfast we have a prayer service out in the hall. Sang tried to get a room for the service, but it will cost money, so we decide to just met in the hall. Because Sang felt called, we used to book David prepared for us. [David was not with us; we would meet him later that evening.] We read 2 Corinthians 1;1-14(NRSV). We read out loud and then share. I find the verse: "Blessed be the God and Father of our Lord Jesus Christ, the Father of mercies and the God of all consolation, who consoles us in all our afflictions, so that we may be able to console those who are in any afflictions with the consolation with which we ourselves are consoled by God."

It is amazing to me how different verses mean more to me now that I have experienced more. I know Jesus was the only one who could heal the pain I felt when Alyssa was born. Sang reminded us that we need to guard ourselves here in Singapore. In this airport we are surrounded by wealth and images of wealth, Swadowski crystals, Pandora bracelets, Mac computers, electronics stories, and so on. Being here, it is easy to forget the suffering in Bangladesh and what we will be doing there. We talked about some of the sacrifices we have already made, like leaving our businesses. Four of the men I'm traveling with own cleaners, and their wives will have extra work because of their trip. What a blessing our devotions was.

I was able to swim. The transit hotel has a pool so I went by myself and swam a hundred laps. It felt so good to swim outdoors. I was the only one in the pool. The water was warm with the sun coming down. I enjoyed the time. I promised Rick I would met him at 1300. He was angry because I wasn't with him. I needed some time alone. We went to eat at a Japanese restaurant, good food. Now we are sitting and talking. I went looking at some things but didn't buy anything because I don't want to carry them. Sarah and I are talking. I really like her.

January 19, 2012 2320

We are in Bangladesh. What a difference I see. The airport was ten times better. The new section was done; there is now a flower garden. We had a welcoming sign. Customs went well; this was the first time it went so fast. All of us made it through without a problem. A young man helped us through. We went through immigration without a problem. The man that gave us a hard time was there. I saw him and thought, Oh, no, here we go, but he did not stop us. David and I noticed the official right away. I told Serena and Christa that was the man. He walked right past me. Director Chang greeted us with a handshake. The director looks well.

We are waiting for vans, and twenty of us pile into the hotel van. Outside the airport the traffic was busy but the hotel was close. We said a short prayer and went to our rooms. Breakfast will be at 0630; we have a wakeup call at 0530. I can smell the pollution already. Hotel staff eager to please. We have picked up David, Christa, and Serena. What a joy it was to see them. It was like meeting old friends. I am glad they are making this journey with us. In our hotel I hear a dripping faucet and the noise of the traffic.

January 20, 2012 0500

Rick and I couldn't sleep any more. We are both stiff, as the bed is hard. Mi Kyong said that our journey was long before we ever got to the people; she is right. I woke up with this thought: some of us met Christ early in our lives, otherwise our journey is early and short. But for some the journey to meet Christ is long and hard. We just don't want him (Jesus). We think we know better. We are able to meet our needs. I met Jesus early in my life. I have great faith and love for Jesus. I do love Jesus, but the walk and my self get in the way. On a lighter note, I am talking to Rick and a mosquito flies into my mouth. Having a mosquito in my mouth in Bangladesh is not what I needed. Once again Eun Jin would laugh because I have my mosquito bracelet on. Our room has a dripping water system (Chinese water torture has a different meaning to me).

January 20, 2012 2130

What a long day. Again the bus ride. I see things differently this year. I know now that I am here because God sent me here. Almost everyone slept on the bus, but I can't sleep. The music helped, playing the i-Pod helped. We had a few close calls. I happened to be looking up at the same time as Frank, and we both gasped. I thought for sure we were going to be hit. I see some improvements but not in the roads. It helped that our trip was on Friday, as there is less traffic, because it's like our Sunday. The director was unable to come with us because Eun Jin's group was delayed, so he sent his local staff. We had a flat tire on our way and got to the compound around 1730. We started to unpack and then ate the local food and some Korean food.

We had a salad, and I asked Toots if a pepper was hot. She said no, so I bit into it. I have never tasted anything so hot. Well, I have something to tease her about. Back to arriving at the compound, the bus pulled in and went around the soccer field. We saw Madame Yoo and Madame Chang. What joy to be with them again. We also saw some of the local workers. We saw Mr. Bablo, Ellie, also Beauty. I also recognized the cook, Beauty's aunt [I would find out later that this was Beauty's mother]. *She was happy to see us. We unpacked. Toots controlled the OR and supplies with helpers. We are going to use the same setup as last year. The patients are already here, so they don't eat. We did devotions this evening. Everyone is tired but still up. Christa and I worked on a plan for the grant research. Her help is so important here. We are looking for equipment and found some new things. The small pulse ox machine I brought is not working, and the one Dr. Pak brought needs a new power source. Well, I'm getting tired and will go to sleep soon. I hope that Sang will get some rest.*

January 20, 2012 0630

First morning. We are all together. Eun Jin and the group arrived around 0130, safe and sound. It's so good that they are with us. Breakfast was done by Toots; she is such a good cook. There is a lot of conversation and confusion. I reflect on the readings and how they fit our journey. I am trying to remember that the first day is the hardest. We must work as a team. I was able to get batteries for the pulse ox machine for Dr. Pak. We are a large group, and I feel a lot more confusion. I have to watch my take charge attitude, that will only get me into trouble. David has us concentrate on things from St. Ignatius:

1) *Become aware of God's presence*
2) *Review the day with gratitude*
3) *Pay attention to your emotions*
4) *Choose one feature of the day and pray for it*
5) *Look toward tomorrow*

What a trip Eun Jin and the group took. They went to Washington DC and missed their flight. Spent the night in Washington. Flew to Dubai and spent eight hours in airport. Poor service on plane. Then when they arrived in Dhaka, there was only one bag handler, and it took two and a half hours through customs. It was also busy because of a Muslim conference. Then the long van ride in the dark and foggy night. I can't think of anything worse than that drive in the night with fog. This group was testing to see if this was a better way to go, because it was cheaper and faster, but they decided that cheaper is not always best.

January 20, 2012 1930

Well, the first day is done. We did nine cases. Christa did the intakes, which was good. She is excited and curious about the patients. We had two cases who returned from last year. One woman and her family remembered me. She was a bad case last year and stayed on the compound for fifteen days. She was all smiles. I saw joy in her eyes. She was more active. I finally remembered her; she couldn't void after the operation and did lots of moaning. What a difference; her prolape had come back, probably because they go back to lifting too soon. Sang told her that he would fix her but she did not want another operation, so she left. Sang told us that she came a long way and asked for money for a rickshaw ride. I guess poverty mentality exists everywhere.

Mrs. Cushim is back, and I was glad to see my friend. We talked and her son is now seven years old and in second grade. He does not go to this school. Our first patient was funny; she started singing in the OR; she fought the spinal, maybe because of not eating. She came to the recovery room, fighting, tossing, and turning. I would later find that she had some mental illness. I had to laugh because she was acting out, and I found out through translation that she was upset because she wanted to eat. So I said she could have three bites of an apple (what she wanted, not what I would give to a patient after an operation). We gave the apple to the mother, and a short time later, I saw what looked like something in her mouth, and guess what it was? I looked at her and said, "You have the apple in your mouth." She smiled because she knew she had been caught. This woman gave me a good laugh. [I laughed because the expression on her face was priceless.]

Eun Jin shared with us at devotions that one of the workers had come up to her and said that they were praying for her father, who has cancer. As Eun Jin was saying this, she was crying.

January 22, 2012

I was too tired to finish writing last night. I went to sleep at 2300 and woke up at 0330 with racing thoughts. My thought are for Beauty, the local nurse. She is overwhelmed with the work. She has no mentor, now. No one she can share work with. I know for me that sharing was an important part of my career. Rick used to say when nurses got together, we would talk about the hospital, and he didn't understand a thing. As I have been writing this journal and have now shared my writings with my daughter, she said I need to define the medical terms as she does not know them (Gina is a teacher).

I know if the hospital is to become a reality, there needs to be nurses with good training. I want to know more about how nurses are trained in

Bangladesh. I would love to help with the training. I say to be careful of what you ask for, as I don't want God to send me here for a long period of time. Sorry, God. I will do what you want me to do. But please, God, don't ask me. Saying that reminds me of Jonah, who didn't want to go to Nineveh. Well, God has taken me on this adventure, and I must remember that this is not about me.

Soo said that in the clinic in Ulipur they saw about twenty women who had prolapses, all wanting help. The few we help here means that there are so many more. I see Sang working tirelessly to help these women. It is so hard to see their condition, and I'm starting to see different types of prolapes. Christa asked if there were stages of prolapes, and Sang said, "Total." I'm sure we could find stages. Maybe someday Sang can present this, when he is not working. We saw one woman whose uterus was all red and inflamed. We could not do surgery on her, too risky. We sent her home with antibiotics to be seen next year after three weeks of treatment.

I am struggling with pain control. We are using Valium with sips of water. I think this has made them more relaxed, but later in the evening, we had complaints of pain because the IVs were dry. One of the hardest parts of this journey has been that I can't be in two places at once and give the nursing care I would give my patients at home. I struggle with this. We only had one patient vomit, a small amount of food, not bad. Bringing the patient in the night before the operation would present a challenge for the local staff, as where would you house them? You don't want to put them with the patients that had an operation, because then I think you will have more pain issues.

January 22, 2012 2115

We are done with day two. We did nine cases. The morning went better, we got a good start because we had five patients prepped for OR. The third patient did some bleeding. Because I work post partum, I have seen hemorrhages, and she was bleeding a lot, large clots. I increased her IV, checked her blood pressure, and told Dr. Lee. He was in the middle of an operation, so he couldn't come. I just kept watching her and stayed with her. I couldn't leave her. The hopelessness you feel. You have no blood, nothing. I would like to tell you I prayed but I would be lying. I watched her till Dr. Lee came out, and he packed her again. The bleeding finally lessened after packing, and she was doing better. [Watching how Dr. Lee packed her was impressive. He used 4 x 4, tied them together with his hands, and pushed the packs inside her uterus and held them till the bleeding stopped.] *We watched her for several hours.*

The rest of the day was busy, but I had Sara and Serena. It's so much better with four nurses, much better. We are still having trouble starting IVs. The patients' hands are so cold. Dr. Pak is starting our IVs. I have started one per day. Beauty is getting tired. I keep telling her to rest. We finished around 1830, just in time for dinner. A hot and spicy chicken dish. We have devotions.

Frank's father died today. How God works things out is that Frank did devotions and spoke in the morning. [By this, I mean Frank spoke in front of the workers and us. He said that his father was not the best father, he didn't treat his mother or the family well. He spoke how he had made peace with this.] *Director Chang talked about how the people of Bangladesh would look at Frank completing the trip. I guess in the Muslim tradition, you would drop everything and leave. So everyone was amazed by Frank's faith. And the fact that Frank and Mi Kyong stayed says a lot to the people of Bangladesh.*

Dr. Hong was discussing medical treatment. I listened to his suggestions but just wanted to clarify why we did something. [He thought maybe we could give patients who will have an afternoon operation some clear liquids. Later I explained that I think that the people look at meals differently than we do and these procedures were new to them.] *Just as I started writing I got word that a patient had a fever. So Serena and I went to visit the patient. Her temperature was only 99.1°F, so we just gave her Tylenol. Then the whole room got Tylenol. If you give to one, you must give to the others. I was glad it was just a false alarm.*

One of the things that happened today was Mrs. Cushim introduced me to her brother. He is a new teacher in the compound. I told him that she was my friend. I told him that he should be good to his sister. I really feel like she is my friend.

January 23, 2011

The day started with a great devotions. We rounded on the patients. The patient that was bleeding we did not send home. We kept her Foley in till later in the day. Sang is afraid of her continuing to bleed. One of the things that surprised me was when I saw Beauty, she grabbed my hand and held it till we got to devotions. Her smile told me she was so glad to see me. She didn't get much sleep during the night. One lady was complaining of pain, so they woke Sang up to see her. The women was screaming and kept everyone up. So he gave her medicine and she felt better.

After devotion we started to get going. We had ten cases scheduled, with an extra. We had a little baby girl (seven months old) who needed a hymenectomy. [Dr. Lee is amazed that these mothers know this at such a young age.] *Her mother left without surgery because the baby was hungry and we didn't get started. Sang examined a woman he suspected had cancer. He could operate on her and debated telling her, but in the end, he told her she needed to see another doctor.*

We also saw a fifteen-year-old married girl who came in with complaints of pain during sex. Sang examined her and said she was developmentally about eight years old; it may be a year before she could have sex, or he could do surgery. Dr. Lee discussed this with her husband. Her husband wanted her to have the surgery, but she didn't want to. They talked for a while and then they left. [I still worry about this girl; was she left, would her husband wait, or would he force himself upon her?] *One again Sang amazed me with his gentle approach with this couple. He said to the husband, "I can see you love her very much."*

Sara helped again today, she cut gowns and undressed patients. Sara is so sweet but she is not a nurse. She is concerned and loving toward the patients. She has a joyful smile and seems to be loving the medical part of the services. Serena has been great. She worked pre-op. Dr. Pak helped start our IVs. Dr. Pak came up with a great idea: using a heating pad to start IVs. It worked! The patients' hand were so cold, really cold. The heating pad made it better. Also he found new tubing, which made it better; this is called creative thinking.

Beauty is giving medications along with Serena. We started about 1030 and had to turn two women away because there was no time. We did four cases before lunch (1430) and had four patients after lunch. The good news is we had prepared them before lunch so the afternoon went better. Tripiti (a retired nurse, who worked with us before) came back for the day. It was good to see her. After lunch, Connie could barely walk down the steps because of hip pain. I went in the OR to help. Serena had gone to the islands. I was there for about thirty minutes before Serena came back. We did one case. Toots runs a tight OR, so I was careful to ask her what she wanted me to do.

One of the things that happened was as the patient was being wheeled out, one of the wheels on the stretcher fell off. Thank God the local people saw this and used the stretcher as a lift. I saw this and went running to help this patient and the staff, so they didn't drop this patient or hurt themselves. The staff tried to fix the stretcher, but this happened twice more. There were only three men to carry the stretcher on the last patient, so Serena and I helped.

Eun Jin had fun with the children, making flowers with pipe cleaners. Rick was able to set up the computer room but there was a computer virus he needed to fix. He is tired and we have had little time to talk, but we will be together on the plane and bus. John L. hurt himself at the soccer game. Mr. Kim painted.

About the stretcher: the wheel needed to be welded. Mr. Young Kim is a welder. God really has a plan. After a good dinner prepared by Frank, we had devotions. I shared something that was hard on me. We knew we wouldn't have enough time to do all the patients, and Sang was in the OR, so I had to examine patients and decide which patients would get surgery. I knew I had seen many prolapses over the years and could decide, but it hit me that my decision would impact their lives. I looked at the women and became overwhelmed. I would hurt some women. I went to prayer. God help me make the right decisions. God, be with me on this job. It's different when you see the suffering. I chose one woman for surgery, and then Sang came out and decided on another, and two women were turned away. I must be absorbing some of this, as I went to God in prayer; before, I would have been confused.

The clinic saw 120 people. John worked through lunch. At devotions, Sang spoke of three ladies returning with prolapes. He explained that in the United States, they would have had hysterectomies. The procedure he is doing is rare and hard to learn, and there will be a paper written on it. He explained about the women's lifestyles; they squat and lift, which they shouldn't be doing for at least four weeks after surgery. He said that the return of the prolapse would spread around to the local people.

Director Chang invited the new members of our group to his office to see the vision of Chilmary Medical Center. I stayed to count pills and talk to Soo, Madame Chang, and Madame Yoo. Soo made me laugh and laugh. I love being with her. Sang went to bed so we didn't round, but Beauty came for pain medication. During devotions, Serena said how she was touched that the children asked for Alex. Serena spoke in front of the group this morning. What a great job she did. [Serena would say how she was a nurse but did not practice, instead she stayed home to raise her family. Three years ago she went back for a refresher class in nursing but was unable to find a job right away. Then Alex got transferred to Singapore, where she is not nursing. God's plan was to take her to Bangladesh, and she would use her nursing skills there.]

January 24, 2012

Happy birthday to me! Happy birthday to me!

Well, another birthday in a foreign land: Bangladesh. I am happy to be here. My friends have already said "Happy birthday" to me. I was too tired to keep writing last night.

January 24, 2012 2200

We are finished; the medical stuff is done, and we will be leaving in the morning. Sang is out in the hall, sorting through supplies and counting for next year. I chose not to be out there so I can write. I am tired but need to do some writing. I had a sheet of paper on which I wrote some thoughts to include, but I can't find it and can't remember what I wanted to write about. The day started with the surgical team going to Ulipur and seeing the worship center that broke ground last year. The director explained that it cost $20,000 to build, and it was sturdy. He showed us the site he saw for the hospital. Right in the middle, the hospital would be three stories. This area is large enough. I told him I saw easy access to the road. Chilmary is ten miles farther and more remote; also, it is closer to the water and I believe more likely to flood. Also he has the leprosy program already there. And the site at Ulipur is more peaceful. The director seemed pleased with what I said. Also in Ulipur, the population is more multicultural (Muslim and Hindu).

I look at my life and never imagined that this area, where I stood the first time I went to Bangladesh, would be the area we were standing and having a conversation about building a hospital. This area had nothing there, and the director was talking about his vision for a leprosy program. I also was amazed that God had taken me to this place, me, a nurse from Detroit, standing in Ulipur, Bangladesh, talking about building a hospital.

January 25, 2012 1830

We left at 0815 am from Chilmary and just arrived at the hotel. The ride was good till Dhaka. We had lunch at the restaurant, the one we went to on the way up. And we only had one potty stop. Again I look outside and saw green, green, and more green. One again I just want to take a rag and wipe the dust from the leaves. It is dirty and very dusty in Bangladesh. I wonder why Bangladesh never became a modern country, because it has all the natural resources: wind, sun, and water. Also it has people. Lots of people.

Eun Jin made a point about her project, wrapping the pipe cleaners and making flowers with the children. I asked her how that went, and she said that some of the children were behind in manual dexterity, and it was difficult. She reminded me that children like Gibson had toys that encouraged manual dexterity.

I am starting to feel the dirtiness of Bangladesh. My jacket is dirty, really dirty. When we travel I see the laundry hanging outside, but clothes still look dirty. It's more than dirt, it's dusty. The air pollution with all the brick makers is so bad. I started to have a little fear on the bus at first, but I put on my head phones and listened to my spiritual music and felt better. Connie was going to sit in one seat, but because of a cracked window, she said, "I'm not sitting by a cracked window."

Compared to the other return trip to Dhaka, this trip was uneventful, except the bus driver missed the street to the hotel. He backed up the bus in the middle of rush hour traffic. I guess no going around the block. We kept hearing a pat on the bus, as the director was giving him directions. Again this was in the middle of rush hour traffic, and there was the director out there. We all had a good laugh about this. Can you imagine, I mean, the middle of rush hour! We had a nice Chinese dinner at the hotel and then devotions on Corinthians, and then it was time to chill. It has been a few days since I have had down time, even for a few hours. Rick is reading and I'm writing.

I need to catch you up on yesterday's activities, as I was tired. For my birthday, Madame Yoo made me a birthday cake; she steamed it. It was like a fruit cake. They put a sign on it (Sue was involved): "Danger: Do Not Touch" in Korean, like I could read it.

January 26, 2012

I am awake at 0400. I fell asleep at 2115. I couldn't keep my eyes open. Today is our day to sleep in, but the bed is so hard and I'm achy, so I decided to write instead. At least it's quiet now. For some reason, there was a worker welding until 2100 next to our room. Well, I never heard that in a hotel before. We were also next to the work station, so we heard the worker phone.

Again, let me catch you up with all the things that have happened. I have a whole list of things. I will write while they are fresh in my mind. On Mr. Kim's project: he was painting Madame Yoo's house, and the local men made a ladder out of bamboo. The funny part about this is that they made a ladder wide enough for two. We watched them work hard constructing it. They used twine. In order to use this ladder, one worker would be on top of the roof, holding the ladder so it wouldn't move. I did see one person climbing the ladder but never two. [I was told that two people did use this ladder; I would have liked to see that.] While I think this was creative, safety is an issue. I never saw Mr. Kim on the ladder. He never tried it. All of the ladders we have seen in Bangladesh have been quite entertaining for us.

*In our conversations with each other over this week, I discovered that three people on this trip had gone to Bible study fellowship with Valerie and Don (Matt and Joanne's daughter and son-in-law) at Woodside Church(.*I have mentioned Joanne before as my water aerobics instructor and Matt was our Bible Study teacher.) *They know Valerie and Don very well. The people from our group are Christa, John Lee, and Serena. What a small world. John said that they joined the group in the study of Revelation after 9/11. I will pass this on to Joanne so she can tell Valerie and Don.*

I love devotions because we get to hear about each other's day. This helps us connect with each other, and because of David's leadership, we connect in a spiritual way. Christa shared with us how she was walking around the compound one day; she was done with intakes and went to the school. She was surrounded by high school girls, much like the picture on the cover of this book. They got to know each other's names, but because of language, they couldn't understand each other. Trying to find things to do, they asked her to sing. She then sang her favorite song, "I Love You, Lord." Christa had no way of knowing that we sang that song on the way to the hospital with Connie after the accident.

Christa has been a great joy on this journey. Sang asked her to come back. You can see her heart. She connected with the people doing intake, and when we left, she was on the bed, holding one woman's hand. That's the part of the trip that is the hardest for me, because I connect to these women with my heart and body language, not with my voice. It's been a learning lesson and sometimes quite frustrating for me. Sara expressed that frustration to me when I asked her if she would be back. She is so eager and was so helpful to us in pre-op and post-op. She did anything I asked. She was always trying to reassure the patients. Sara has a joyful spirit and must decide if she has a heart for service. I am blessed to have this time getting to know her.

On January 24, 2012, I woke up at 0200 and couldn't sleep. I heard a noise outside but it was not the call to prayer, so I think that because we were here, there was some chanting against us. We asked the director about it, and he said that there was a Muslim revival meeting the last few days and that is what we heard. I felt better about that.

On my birthday, Toots made a special dinner: papaya soup and noodles. The Filipinos believe that having noodles on your birthday will give you a long life. Toots knows I love her noodles. The fact she made them for me is special. Toots's heart is great, and her meals are great too. She is a special friend I cherish. She is so proficient in the OR, and her skills are so great. Because of this, it would be hard to replace her. She would be mad at me for writing this, but I saw that she was more stiff and had a harder time walking after working this year. She is sixty-six years old; it is amazing that she can do all of this work and cook. She has more energy than most of us.

On the last day of surgery, January 24, Dr. Pak and Serena, along with Beauty, did pre-op. Dr. Hong did OR. I love working with Dr. Pak. He is very patient. Because of the previous three days, we knew what we should do, so I didn't need to go in pre-op; the three of them had it covered. Christa had done some intakes the night before, so that went easier. Finally, on the last day, I got this idea that we should have an undressing room. Undressing the women is hard. They are nervous and fearful. Being checked by a man is overwhelming to them. Many women will not open their legs for an exam. Because of their fear and nervousness, it takes awhile to undress them, and this holds up the operation. I finally suggested we use the supply room. This was a better idea. I wish I had thought about it three days before. Well, better late than never.

We were in Ulipur (sorry, I'm going back); John, a lawyer, gave his testimony. He did a great job. He talked about Detroit and the decreasing population and Detroit's problems. He talked about his first trip to Ulipur and the children and what they looked like. He told them of the changes they had made and said that the children looked healthier. Then Sang introduced us to the staff. When Sang introduced me, he said, "I love her." And then he acknowledged this in Rick's presence. Hearing those words and knowing the journey we have come through is so soothing. We are truly brother and sister in Christ. [I do feel Sang's love for me when I am around him, and I truly thank God for bringing him and Soo into my life.]

Since I have been going to Bangladesh, I have developed a friendship with Mrs. Cushim. This year we had time to talk, but not as much as I would have liked. She had her duty to her children. We were able to talk for a short while, and she told me her mother had a prolapes repaired. She also said that her mother was forty-five, and I asked her how old she was. She said thirty years old. We also talked about her son. She said he has epilepsy and that she would be talking him to a neurologist in Dhaka in about three months. I told her that I would pray for her.

After we were done with all the surgeries, the compound had a ceremony with dancers. Bangladesh dancers are similar to the dancers I have seen in the Philippines. The girls were in beautiful native costumes. Their hands were painted. The outfits were similar to what I have seen in Indian movies and from my friends' pictures. There were two sets of dancers, some were high school girls. [Like the dance I saw in the Philippines, they did a pole dance with the boys holding the bamboo sticks and the girls dancing between them. I was really surprised to see a similar dance in two different countries.] *The second and third grades presented a performance, this was Mrs. Cushim's class. It was so cute with music and dancing.* [Eun Jin would tell me later that the song was "We Shall Overcome."] *I could see Mrs. Cushim directing them. They had signs that said, "Doctors, Nurses, Engineers." This performance was so tender and enjoyable. Mrs.*

Cushim removed all of the children because of the noise [excitement]. *I could not be more proud of Mrs. Cushim. She is a good teacher; her leadership skills show. Eun Jin told me that early in the day, they judged the art contest. They had an assembly in the gym. Because of what I was doing in OR, I didn't get to see it. Last year I enjoyed this.*

I was grateful for my leadership skills (Rick calls me "Miss Full Charge") because of something that happened. We were having stretcher problems again. The wheel kept falling off, probably because of the road it must travel: bumps, hills, dirt, and bricks. I had three patients in the recovery room. Sang was working fast today. I was getting ready to move one. I looked outside and the stretcher was just to the top. I heard the men were working on it. I was trying to take care of the patients, so I couldn't watch every minute to see if it was back in use. The next thing I know, I have a fourth patient with no place to put her. I was shocked and wondered what we would do with her.

All of a sudden Rupal (our transporter) is angry and loud voices are heard. My patient is left outside by herself while families and onlookers are observing the scene. I said in a calm tone amidst the angry voices, "Let's take care of the patient and we'll figure this out." No response. So again, "Move the patient into the other room and let's figure out what to do." They finally listened to me and moved the patient. After she was moved, I heard small wooden benches (the kind you sit on) being moved into that room. I walked in to see the benches with blue pads on, looking like a bed. "We will put her here," was what the staff told me. Then I saw them all talk and they decided that they would keep the patient on the stretcher rather than move her. Let her recover on the stretcher. I thought that this was a great idea, as it meant less moving. The only thing that meant was Beauty couldn't go to lunch till she was moved, because now we had two rooms for recovering patients.

This solution worked and it was good problem solving. I praised the staff for their thinking this through. I hope this is because we have been here before, but I'm not sure. I know how hard this is on the staff, as we are understaffed. They are lifting way too much and working long hours. Fortunately the stretcher held up for a few more patients. I bring my treats for them just as a way of saying thanks and I care. We are a team. One day I gave Beauty a treat, and she shared it with me. We are getting to know each other better. Beauty is a great nurse with many challenges ahead of her. I encouraged her. On the final day we found her sleeping, and it was hard to wake her up. [Four nights with little sleep will do that!]

Dr. Stark's idea for a potty chair was not received as well as planned. Mr. Song built a private area for the women to use. We never showed the staff. We showed Beauty but she didn't encourage it. Finally, on the last day we suggested the women use it rather than going outside. The women did use it; I'm not sure how new ideas go over with the women. We also need to find a way to clean it between patients. [I plan to figure this out for next time.]

One of the things that happened on January 24 was that we ran out of Foley bags (for catheters). Sang decided we didn't need them. We would remove the Foleys in the recovery room, keep the catheters using clean techniques, and hope the patients voided (urinated); we could catheterize them later if they didn't void. We didn't discuss this plan before, but I remembered last year when I catheterized someone in the dark in the post-op unit. I found myself not liking the idea. I found myself resentful, especially when we found leg bags in the storage room and attached them to two patients. I told Sang about the leg bags, and he still said to take the catheter out, the patient will move better. I really didn't want to do this. He said when they are able to move their legs, then remove the Foley. Of course this was after I sent two patients with the bags to the post-op unit. This now meant I had to go to post-op room, keeping the catheters sterile (clean) in case we needed them, removing them in front of people, crawling on hands and knees on the patient's bed.

I was a little frustrated and was trying to share my frustration with Beauty through Madame Yoo. I am now grateful she did not translate what I said. We need to look like we work well with each other. I did what Dr. Lee told me to do. We would deal with the outcome later. We did rounds that evening, and the patients had not gotten up to void. We woke Beauty up and told her to get them up and have them void. All the women voided, and we did not have to catheterize anyone. Dr. Lee was right; none of the women needed to be catheterized. [Once again I reminded myself that I can have a bad attitude and am not perfect. Because I use my coworkers sometimes to release frustrations, I felt I could do that with Beauty. I was wrong; I was to show her how a Christian should act. I was wrong. Thank you, God, for the lesson.]

Along with the performance, Frank did a video presentation from England and from Grameen Shakti about the new inventions being done in Bangladesh for energy. Then he presented things he already saw that the compounds of Chilmary and Ulipur needed to improve. Frank promised a commitment to help them change some things. Frank gave them the evaluation of what he saw and a promise that he would help.

We later met as a group to discuss with the director how the Free Medical Services event went. This was our time for evaluations. *What did we think about having twenty-two people in the group? Everyone was silent. We asked Madame Yoo and Madame Chang for input. They said that having so many people is hard on the staff. The director said that three things are important for the group to succeed:*

1) *The senders must be healthy.*
2) *The group must be spiritually healthy.*
3) *The assigned place must be healthy.*

The director said that in his experience twelve people is the idea number of people. Fifteen is the most number of people. His suggestion was maybe a maintenance services, medical services, educational services with specific goals. We all took this in.

Early in the day on January 24, I told Coach David that I thought Eun Jin should be a facilitator for medical services. He said that she would have to go to school. That evening, as we were going through our discussion time, Eun Jin shared how she does well when she is working to give free medical services but has no patience when she is at work. Dr. Hong then said, "You know the solution, became a facilitator." David and I just looked at each other because of our earlier conversation.

After everyone was finished, I told the group about this book. I was nervous because I wasn't sure how people would take this news. I stated the facts and told them to tell me if they did not want me to use their names. The room was silent, with no response. We closed with a prayer. When we walked outside Serena said, "I didn't know you were writing a book." As we were walking after rounds, the director hugged me and thank me. I had told the group that I would only take expenses I incurred for writing the book and the rest will be donated for Chilmary Medical Center. Rick joked to the group that "only 10 percent of the movie rights would go to Chilmary Medical Center." He got a laugh. I can't see this writing being that good, but whatever God has planned. Sang was surprised.

January 27, 2012

We woke up and rounded early in the morning after breakfast. All the women are doing well. Sang asked me to lead prayers for the women as we leave. It's hard for me to pray on the spot. I'm so used to rote prayers and can't seem to say long prayers. Public praying is hard for me. I am really not sure why. I believe it's my Catholic background. I grew up praying quietly in church by myself. The only public prayers were repetitive prayers. I am also a person who likes life planned. I like to know ahead of time. I feel like I need to prepare. I need to remember that God wants prayers from the heart. God wants our hearts. I need to ask the Holy Spirit for guidance on this one. My fears also might have something to do with my insecurities, though I shouldn't have insecurities with prayers.

We say good-bye to each other. It's cold outside. Beauty holds my hand as we walk. I have wondered if she will offer the watch back (I had given Beauty my watch earlier to take heart rates because she did not have a watch and I felt every nurse should have a watch). *She does not. Because of the language difference, she may not have understood I would want it back (or it may be what the director has told us, that when you give something to the Bengali people, they expect something from you). Beauty's mom (the woman who cooks and cleans for us) hugs us. She is happy, I believe because her daughter will have it better and because of the way we treat her daughter. I am grateful to give Beauty the watch.*

We say good-bye to Madame Yoo and Madame Chang. It's always hard to say good-bye to them. I love both of these women. What joy I see in them. I can only imagine some of the struggles they go through. Both of them have given their lives for the people of Bangladesh. I wonder how they can be so self-sacrificing. They both have simple means, both have much compassion, both must suffer from loneliness, but at least they have each other. There is a sense of peace about them, and I think it's because they are following God's plan for their life. I will continue to pray for these dear, sweet, godly women, and I can't wait till I see them again.

We talk, sleep, snack, and make pipe cleaner rings on the bus. I tried to make the rings but am not very good, so I give up. I sense Rick is a little tense, so I sit with Connie for a little while. When I move back, Rick is less tense. We stop at the same restaurant as we ate at on the way up. Except for Dhaka, the trip back is quicker. Once again the music helps me relax. Not only are there so many near misses with the cars, rickshaws, and busses, but there is the honking for passing, which goes on constantly. After a while this is very hard on the nerves. You hear the honking, speed up, then slow down for speed bumps or other rickshaws, bikes, or motorcycles. We spend ten hours on the trip down. Once again I see what the people live with. I wonder if I will ever get used to what I see out the window. I hope not. I am starting to recognize places. I kind of know how much longer. The bus passes our street, so Director Chang gets out of the bus and stops traffic, and in the middle of rush hour, we back up a large bus. The director is a little crazy. But despite this we are able to back up the bus and make the turn.

Finally at the hotel. We have a meal there. The Bangladesh staff is attentive. We sing and have devotions. The director makes sure that the door is closed. He would tell us later that there had been some bad press in Dhaka, accusing Chilmary Medical Center of trying to make Christians out of the whole nation. On some level, that's true, but not in the way people think. People have to be able to see and think for themselves. Our God is not a pushy God. God sent Jesus to save us, but he gave us freedom to choose him. The staff of Chilmary Medical Center Dhaka have been suffering because of these accusations.

The hotel room is dirty. Most of Bangladesh has this dirty film on it; even bleach wouldn't help. We sleep on a hard bed. The beds in the compound are softer than these. I am really not complaining, just informing you of what things are like. We hear welding noise right outside our door. The staff is talking, but I am too tired not to fall asleep.

We slept in to 0800, have breakfast, and then we are on the road again. Connie asked to see the front of Apollo Hospital, as she had never seen it. (This was the hospital that Connie went to after the accident) *The director took us there, and from the outside it was a beautiful hospital, very Western. The hospital was established by an Indian company. We went into the hospital, and in the entrance was a pharmacy, outpatient department, snack and drink shop, cashier, and elevators to take you to the eleventh floor. John took a picture of the services they offered. The lobby had the names of thirty-one doctors, with all kinds of specialties. I would have loved to see postpartum, OB, and NICU, but there was a security guard at the elevators, so going up to see them was impossible.*

Connie, on the other hand, was determined to see Dr. Ali, the doctor who had treated her. She went looking for him, and when he heard she was there to see him, he left his patients and examined Connie; he looked up her CT scan and was glad to see her. He also told her that he was interested in building a hospital and knew officials in the government who could help. Soo was so excited when she got back on the bus, but Sang was the one who told us. He was also excited. Sometimes I feel like I need to pinch myself and am amazed that I am a small, very small part of this.

I believe Satan meant to stop us from coming back, but our love for God and the people of Bangladesh kept us coming back. I am glad Connie got to hear those words, as I believe this is her last trip. Seeing Dhaka was good for me, because I could see the progress the people of Bangladesh are making; there were definitely more cars and traffic jams where you only move inches.

To understand why Connie's injury is so amazing, you have to know a little bit of bone structure. The femoral head is in a socket in the pelvis, and cartilage and fluid is around it. The head of the femur pushed through some of this, and normally a doctor would open up the patient in OR and put screws in, and the patient would require six months of treatment. The doctors felt that because Connie was immobilized in the ambulance for ten hours, some of the tissue repaired itself. Dr. Ali had planned to do an ORIF (open reduction, internal fixation) of the femur, but something told him to do a closed reduction. He could not explain his actions other than that he had a feeling about this.

He pulled on her leg, and everything fell into place. Connie spent six to eight weeks in this private pay hospital, and the bill was paid anonymously. She left for the Philippines six weeks later. Dr. Ali did not want her to go, but she begged, and that's sometimes how God works. Connie had paid for a nephew to train as a physical therapist in the Philippines. She joked that she had her own physical therapist to take care of her.

After the trip to the hospital, the director took us to Aragon's, a local Bangladesh store, but because of the stop at the hospital, we only had thirty minutes for shopping. Thirty minutes? Come on. Who gives women thirty minutes? I had the advance because I had been there before. I wanted to buy a scarf, but by accident I opened a sari. The store had just a few scarves, so then I went looking for shawls. I bought nine scarves for the girls who worked for me for $88. Rick bought a nice shirt. After this we went to a local Korean restaurant with great food. We had soup, salad, appetizers, rice, and a main dish; I had ice cream, very good ice cream with an almond taste.

We got back in the van and went to the music school. I was disappointed because the building the school was in before was much nicer. We did see a wonderful performance by the teachers of the school. There were three Korean teachers who will be going back to Korea soon. The concert was awesome. A Bengali teacher played a violin along with a Korean teacher. The performance I liked best was the Bengali students singing "Mother of Mine" and a Korean song. They were really good. The one thing I saw was joy on their faces. They were enjoying singing for us, but they really enjoyed singing. This performance was first rate, and I know this because my daughter is in music and I sat through many of her performances. They were good, there was joy in this performance, and this was a great ending to our visit. It really gave me hope for Bangladesh.

After the concert, it was time for the first group of us to leave to catch their plane. It's always hard when we start breaking up, as we have been so close. Saying good-bye is hard. Most of that group I will see at home. For some reason, Frank was wearing black, which was the same color as the male Bengali singers, so someone told him he should be Elvis, so Frank started to perform for us. The singers stayed and enjoyed the antics. Then we toured the Chilmary Medical Center's office and the director's living arrangements in Dhaka. First of all, the music rooms are on the sixth floor, and staff offices, along with the director's living quarters, are on the seventh floor. This building has no working elevator. I get mad when people don't want to give to the foreign lands because they think that the director of programs will get rich; they wonder what the money is going toward. I tell them they should do their homework and find out about the organization. I also tell them that I have seen where the director lives, and it's modest: bedroom, kitchen, and bathroom. There is a balcony outside where they chose to put a driving range for hitting golf balls. The view is pretty, but I wouldn't get too close to the edge.

We went to another Korean restaurant with the Chilmary Medical Center teachers. We had a good time, but Rick was mad at me because I stopped him from telling them that Mark is overweight. I told him a few times that this bothered me. Rick was quiet for a few minutes and then better.

After dinner, we went to the airport. I don't know why there are always so many people standing outside the door of the airport. This makes it so hard for passengers to get in. I always feel a little intimidated and vulnerable when we go in. I knew what bag was mine this time because I put white lace around it. We got through check-in and immigration easily this time. I went to the book store and got a map and a Bengali language book. I will still keep trying to learn the language. There are lots of mosquitoes in the airport. The airport at Dhaka has improved; it looks more dressed up with flowers and new floors. At the airport, we said good-bye to the director, promising to see him again. I was tired and slept on the plane. Singapore Air is a nice airline. I was so tired I didn't eat.

January 27, 2012

We arrive in Singapore at 0445. The hotel lets us check in early so we all go and take a nap; after we wake up, we go to breakfast/lunch. It feels good to sleep in a soft bed with clean sheets. The room has a king size bed, refrigerator, and recliner. We walk in the hot sun for miles and then eat. There is confusion, as everyone wants different things. Toots, Connie, Rick, and I choose local food, and then later Soo, Sang, and Dr. Pak join us. We eat traditional Singapore food; the food is very good. Rick and I then take Sara to the river front. She enjoys it, but she is too hot. We meet up with Song, Mr. Nine, Mr. Kim, and Mr. Yang, and they go on a boat ride. They tell Sara not to hang out with a married couple (They felt a married couple should have time alone). *Rick and I go back and get Connie, and then we go shopping at Lucky Plaza. We find some good deals. Connie buys some expensive yellow and red jade earrings for her nieces. We decide not to go back to the room but to meet where we are having dinner. So Rick, Connie, and I find the place thirty minutes early and wait. We have good food and enjoy the time with Christa, Alex, and Serena. We say our good-byes.*

One of the things we would see in Singapore is trucks loaded with Bengali men. These men would go to Singapore for work. They would be away from their families, trying to provide for their families. Just like in the United States; we do what we have to do to get by.

January 28, 2012

We are up at 0230 to catch our flight. These flights are long: seven hours from Singapore to Tokyo. Right after we land, we board the plane to Detroit [no time for noodles]. This is a very long flight. I am coughing and feel chilled. Rick is restless.

January 30, 2012

Well, it's been two days since we have been home. We arrived at 1230 and then went to the Korean Methodist church for a short prayer. We went to a Korean restaurant and then went home after dropping Toots and

Connie off. Our daughter visited us with the grandchildren, but by 1730, I was sleeping in the chair. I went to bed from 1730 till 0430 with a few bathroom breaks. It felt so good to sleep in a soft bed. You really appreciate your own bed when you go away and return. On January 29, we went to Rick's sister's house in Canada for her sixtieth birthday. Today we are still catching up with mail and watching the grandchildren, and I went to exercise at the gym. There are always things I forgot to write about till a few days later; sometimes I just don't have the time or energy to write.

[One of the things I forgot to write about is what I call Chilmary Medical Center's success story: Ellis. He is one of the people I have seen on my trips to Bangladesh. He interprets for us, though sometimes he has a hard time understanding us. We had some down time, so I got a chance to hear his story. He worked at Chilmary Medical Center as a young man as a security guard. He was able to save money and went to school. He has a bachelor's degree and went on to get a master's degree. I was impressed; we have worked together before, but we never got this personal. I am quite fond of him. He has a great sense of humor and is so helpful. When we left, I felt the need to hug him but I have learned to ask the men of Bangladesh before hugging them. Ellis said it was okay but I noticed that he did not hug back. If he would have hugged back, that would have been improper. Someday maybe I will learn what is proper, nevertheless I felt the need to hug this man, who I have come to love and look forward to seeing again.]

I have two stories I need to share. The first one is a conversation that went on in the evening with Frank, Mi Kyong, Rick, Eun Jin, the director, and me. We were talking about children. Mi Kyong had already shared with us that her daughter had a son when she was eighteen years old. That evening she shared how hard it had been, raising a grandson. Both of their daughters are single mothers. One of their daughters is not doing well. After we shared stories, Director Chang told us about his life. [This was the first time we would hear his story from his mouth.] *His father was a spiritual advisor. The director had prayed to get into the Seoul National University. He did not get into the university, even with good grades and top honors. Because he did not get into the university, he decided that there was no God. Not only that, he became very rebellious. He saw no value in religion. His rebellion included kicking in the door of his father's organization and yelling at his father publicly, saying, "Don't believe him."*

He went out drinking and partying for seven years. During this time his parents would pray for him, sometimes without stopping. One day he was so drunk that he fell to the ground in a stupor outside his parents' house. His neighbor found him, and he told her to go away. He woke because he felt something warm on his face; it was tears falling on his face. He recognized the tears as the tears of his parents.

Those tears caused a change in his life. He went back to school and trained to become a director. He asked God to take him to the poorest of the poor, and that was how he came to Bangladesh. The director's words were meant to give Frank, Mi Kyong, Rick, and myself hope. [I think that these words are meant to give hope to all parents with children not acting like God wants them to act. When I see what one person accepting what God has told him to do has done, and when I see what the director's parents' prayers did, I know there is hope.] *Today, the director is devoted to serving God through the people of Bangladesh.*

The other story occurred on the bus ride in Dhaka. Frank and Mi Kyong were sharing how they met, and then Soo started sharing how she met Sang. She met him through a blind date (this is the same way I met Rick). The couple who arranged this did not tell Soo she was meeting someone. The couple who introduced them did not stay for dinner; they made excuses and left, leaving her and Sang together. The next day, Sang gave her something he had written: it was a draft of his plans for his life; he told her to keep it.

It turned out for Sang, it was love at first sight. Soo was unsure, and Sang sensed that he was pushing and asked for the draft back. He would visit her at her parents' home; knowing that they had dogs. Sang would bring dog biscuits, so he made friends with the dogs. [This part of the story is so cute and clever.] *He would also visit with her family. Soo's family fell in love with him. Soo's grandmother said, "We should keep this one because even the dogs like him."*

Eventually, Sang won Soo's heart, and he gave her back the draft of his life plan. On their honeymoon, a family friend booked a suite for them to share, but Soo told Sang that she didn't want to start their married life like this, knowing that the hotels were filled. They found a place they could afford. Later Sang took Soo back to the hotel, and they got the suite, which they now could pay for.

I went to three churches on January 29: the Catholic church, a non-denominational church, and the Korean Methodist church. Some people may think this is a horrible thing, but I love what God does in my life. I'm always amazed when I hear things at one church that I hear at another church. I heard a song at the Korean church that I knew: "Only a Step to Jesus." I have thought about the many steps I have taken in my life. I am so profoundly blessed that many of my steps have been next to Jesus. I am grateful that, like the "Footprints" poem, when there was only one set of footprints, Jesus was carrying me. I can't imagine my life without Jesus.

We have been studying the gospel of John this year. I know most of the stories of the Bible, having spent twelve years in Catholic school, but this year I am getting to know Jesus differently. A whole different world has opened up to me. I asked Jesus into my heart once again after asking him into my heart about eight years ago on a road in Bangladesh; it was one step.

How about you? It's not hard. It's "Only a Step to Jesus." He's waiting for you to take that step. I hope you take that step.

I believe the word "history" says something about God's story. The very word says "HIS Story." The Bible tells us the story of God and his people (us). God is a faithful God. He loves us and is trustworthy. What I have written is the story of myself, Rick, Dr. Lee, Eun Soo, the director, Connie, Toots, Eun Jin, and many others, but most of all it's the story of the people of Bangladesh, who I now call my friends.

I heard a speaker just say something that I needed to hear as I finished my story: "Jesus is the ultimate author. Let him write your story." I know he has written my story and continues to do so.

Women of Bangladesh

I have seen you. I have watched you work in the rice fields.
I have seen you wash clothes in water unfit to be standing in.
I have seen just your eyes because you were dressed in a burka as we met.
I have seen you holding a dying child, desperately looking for help.
I have seen your fear as you trust strangers to "fix" you.
I have seen you trying to make your daughter's life better.
I have seen you walking in thin sandals.
I have seen you aged before your time.
I have seen the hair that needs to be combed and washed.
I have seen your daughters care for you.
I have touched you. I have held your hand.
I have helped you get undressed.
I have wiped your tears.
I have tried to calm your fears.
I have been carried by you.
I have laughed with you; you have laughed at me.
I have learned from you; I hope you have learned from me.
I want for you what I have now: peace in my heart.
I am forever changed because of the time I have spent with you.

CHAPTER 11:

I Don't Know What I'm Doing Here (Rick's Chapter)

Additional musings by Richard Augustiniak

It's January 2009. I'm in a jumbo jet headed to Narita Airport, Tokyo, Japan. We will stop there briefly, then on to Singapore and finally to Dhaka. In case you don't know this, that is the capital city of Bangladesh (you know, the "Concert for Bangladesh," that place). Now if you had asked me which hundred places I would really like to go before I die, Bangladesh would not have been on the list. So as we make our way across the Pacific Ocean, the thought crosses my mind occasionally: "What am I doing here?" Don't misunderstand me. I have always supported helping the poor, and I have always admired the people who have given of themselves and traveled to remote corners of the globe to help needy people. I just never saw myself as one of them. I had dreamed of traveling to Mars or Venus or going on a five-year mission with Captain Kirk, but going to Bangladesh never entered my muddiest dreams.

Let me give you a little background. My wife, Vicki, has been to Bangladesh several times before. This was something she had wanted to do for many years. I can still remember the day she told me she was going for the first time. She was excited, nervous, and a little scared. I was encouraging, supportive, and glad I wasn't going. (See, I was supportive of helping the poor and downtrodden and the people who go to help them.) When she arrived for her first trip, there wasn't much there. A few buildings, a start of a school, and a makeshift clinic were all that existed. Let's fast forward a few years. Now they have a grade school and a middle school, offices, a sewing school, real living quarters, and computer training school in the Chilmary Medical Center. Being a database programmer at that time, I was targeted (I mean encouraged) to join the team. I resisted at first. They kept suggesting I come along, and I kept coming up with reasons not to. Eventually, when I was in a weak moment, they got me to agree in principle that maybe I would join them someday and maybe someday I would be able to help.

Computer class in Bangladesh

I might just as well have said yes at that point. Next thing I know I'm getting my visa and immunization shots, attending meetings, and learning Bengali (or is it Bangla?), the native language (still haven't learned it, probably never will; I have a hard enough time with the queen's English).

So there I was, the intrepid traveler, way outside my comfort zone, on a journey I had never realized I would be on, in a country I hadn't envisioned I'd ever be in, doing the kind of computer work that had never entered my muddiest dreams back when I decided to change careers twenty-two years ago. God has a sense of humor.

That was my mind-set on my first trip. It's different now. I'm different, I guess. In my previous excursions into Bangladesh, I felt more like a tourist. I was a tourist, just a tagalong, an extra pair of hands if needed. My observations are from the perspective of seeing a new country—new, meaning I hadn't been there before—seeing these people with their strange customs, strange dress, strange beliefs, and even stranger food (I still don't like the curry). This is my third trip as I write this, and it is different. By this time I was participating. I came with a purpose, a direction, a vision, something far beyond myself (oh, get off the pedestal). I came back to Bangladesh to help, to give. I came back to help my friends.

Now that being said, with three trips under my belt, I have made some observations. These are things that interest me, or maybe disturb me, or just plain blow me away.

Who turned off the heat: One of the pleasures of traveling, especially in the winter, is the possibility of a break from the cold weather. Here in Michigan, it was relatively snow free but still cold. I don't relocate (flee) to Florida or other warm spots during the winter months like some folk do (snowbirds, they're called). I just tough it out. My blood is thinner and my skin is not as tough as it used to be, so I feel the cold more. This type of travel does give us a short break from the cold, allowing us to pass through warmer climates. Our work involves lots of traveling. So as we set out on this trip to Bangladesh, that was one of the pleasures I was looking forward to. It just didn't happen this year. There was a short layover in Singapore, where it was hot, in the upper 80s, but we didn't stay very long. We were just hanging out between flights. When we finally arrived in northern Bangladesh (thirty hours by plane and bus), it was cold. Not a whole lot warmer than what we had left behind. Not what I expected. It didn't slow us down or keep us from accomplishing what we went for: caring for those who need help, and that is what we did. It's warming to the heart to reach out and help others in need, as God has directed us. My heart wasn't cold, but my hands and feet were. (What was that about global warming?)

Flying: First off, I enjoy flying. I still get a rush from the takeoff. I eat all the food, drink all the drinks, read all the catalogs and flight magazines, and just have fun. There is the hassle of the security checks, but that is for our safety and the safety of our fellow passengers. I have flown to New York, Chicago, Texas, Florida, Tennessee, and Hawaii. I have even been to England and Israel. These trips require a dedicated spirit, a true sense of commitment. We are in the air for fifteen hours on the initial leg of our trek. That gets us to Narita, Japan. We have to disembark with our carry-on luggage, go through the security check again, and get right back on the same plane. They do take that time to replenish the food, clean the plane, and freshen up the air some. I mean, we have been in the air for about fifteen hours, packed in close quarters, so the plane needed a breather and so did we.

The race to get through security and back to our gate so we could sit and wait for the next leg of our travels provides some much needed stretching. We can shop a bit, but it doesn't do much good on our outbound trip. We could buy some gum (forget that, can't chew gum in Singapore) or a pen or some pencils from Japan for the grandkids. We had walked the aisles as the hours slowly passed to keep our blood circulating and leg cramps at a tolerable level. It broke up the monotony of reading *War and Peace* for the third time.

I forgot to mention that we all had one carry-on that all of our clothing and personal items for ten days were crammed into. That's not much room. We each checked two bags full of supplies. So I didn't have a lot to read. I can read a lot in fifteen hours, especially if there isn't anything else to do. I usually don't care for the in-flight movies that they show. Either they are violent or stupid, or worse, they show a sitcom that is insulting to the intelligence of any creature smarter than a fruit fly. If by some quirk of fate they have something somewhat entertaining or interesting, you might as well enjoy the silence or learn to read lips because the headphones don't work right. (I'm such a whiner.) So there wasn't much else to do except read. You can only read the catalogs in the pockets so many times. I survived (used an e-Book reader later, had thirty books with me).

So now we are back on the plane again for another seven hours, heading to Singapore. We will spend some time in Singapore, usually eight to ten hours on this leg and a day or so on the return trip. Then we get back on a plane to Dhaka, Bangladesh, another four to five hours.

The land of dark: We arrived at night, so I couldn't get a feel for the city from the air. The airport was dirty, just plain dirty. We had passed through Narita and Singapore airports, where you could eat off the floors, walls, or ceiling. Those places sparkled. Dhaka Airport was grubby. We stood in line with our luggage; we each had two huge bags full of medical supplies waiting to go through customs. This took forever. Other customs checkpoints do everything online; here, it's all done by hand. Other customs personnel were businesslike yet pleasant. These customs officials were most unpleasant; nobody smiled, nobody was kind; we got the feeling we were not welcome. Not a good first impression. Got through that and headed for the vans to take us to our hotel. Outside the airport fence, there is this mass of people. There are thousands of them. They're not there to pick up family or friends, like we would see at home. They are looking for a handout, most of them; many don't have anything else to do or any place else to go, and they set up make-shift camps. Fires are burning all over the place. I am seeing firsthand the poverty I had only heard of. We load up the vans and head to the hotel.

Not the Ritz: We spent the night in a local hotel. It seemed to be clean, and we were welcome there. There weren't enough rooms for all of us, so we crowded in where we could, men's rooms and women's rooms. The last two trips, Vicki and I had a room to ourselves. It is so hard to describe the dripping shower, the rust stains on the shower wall, broken tiles, and piecemeal plumbing. Hard beds, questionable linens, and lumpy pillows greeted us. At least there was a Western-style toilet that was some comfort, as these are rare in the route we will travel. I have checked, and there isn't a Ritz in Bangladesh, so you needn't bother looking.

Of vans and luggage: Next morning we begin the next stage of our voyage. We have already been traveling for twenty-plus hours, not without rest and some stops along the way, but it has been tiring. The longest trip we have had up to this point was a vacation in Hawaii. Ten hours with lots of sun and food and beaches waiting for us at the end of that trip. Not the case here. We loaded up the vans with twenty-three bags of medical supplies, all strapped to the top, except for a few we crammed in with us. I was kind of glad for the bag behind me and my wife, since we were in the back of the van, right in front of the gas tank. I shudder to think of what would have happened if we were rear ended. It was crowded, but it was only for a short trip. Ten hours, I believe they told me. My first trip to Bangladesh we traveled in these twelve-passenger vans. On subsequent trips we used the large touring bus with storage underneath, and for a very good reason, which I talk about later.

Two-lane blacktop: My wife had told me about this part of the trip, as she had experienced it, but there are some things you just have to see for yourself. I should point out that the city of Dhaka has 12 million people living in it. Well, that morning it seemed that all of them were out on the roads, headed somewhere. I have never experienced congestion of that magnitude anywhere, not anywhere, not in New York, Detroit, or San Francisco. There are no traffic signals, except one by the airport (by my third trip they had added two more). There is nobody directing traffic. Random chaos, with a good dose of pandemonium, just begins to describe the masses of people milling around, yet somehow intent on getting someplace. In our country, we have a system for dealing with a four-way stop. Everyone gets their turn, but not here. Everyone is first. We work our way out of the city. To the residents here and our driver, it's just another day.

The dwellings that line the road are the same as the ones in the city. There are some tall buildings in Dhaka, yet in between them and behind them there are tent-like dwellings and shacks, sometimes nothing more than some poles with some rags and wood hanging on them. Store fronts seem to occupy the rest of the cityscape. There are a couple of factories where they make clothing, some office buildings, and the airport. The rest is shacks and lean-tos. So when we leave the city, the scene is pretty much the same. I had thought that when we were free from the city congestion, we would speed up a bit. Well, we did but not without cost.

Picture this. We are on a two-lane highway, one for each direction, and everything travels along this road, the only road that leads to the Chilmary area; there are no expressways here. This road and many like it make up the transportation system. It is used by everyone, since it connects all the villages in the region. This particular road is used by pedestrians, pedestrians with cows, pedestrians with goats, and pedestrians with burdens on their heads or backs. We see bikes and bikes with carts on the back with big heavy loads on them. Loads of bricks, sticks, corrugated steel, straw, and bamboo are carried by this method on this road, and of course there are rickashaws (more on that later). The road was also traveled by three-wheeled taxis, trucks, military vehicles, and busses.

Now this type of caravan would travel along at the speed of the slowest vehicle. The only way to make any headway is to keep passing the slower traffic, which meant pulling into the other lane, speeding up to pass, and then getting back into your lane before the oncoming traffic reaches you. Now the oncoming traffic is doing the same thing. This caused many heart-stopping moments as we narrowly missed the oncoming vehicles. The stress was unbelievable. Imagine yourself on a roller coaster ride that has one purpose: to scare the living daylights out of you, to literally make your heart stop in sheer terror. That usually lasts for just a few seconds. This went on for hour after hour. Your body is tense the whole time. At the rest stops, you are exhausted. Our drivers, thank God, were very skilled, and this was a normal drive for them. When I returned home, rush hour never bothered me again.

Now what is a rickashaw? We are still on the two-lane blacktop. We have left the city, although I'm not sure when. Rickashaws, lots of them, carrying people and sometimes whole families. You might ask, what is a rickashaw? It is a cart pulled or pedaled by a person carrying other people. Very similar to a rickshaw in appearance and function; however, after several attempts to correct this person I know that the correct pronunciation is *rickshaw*, we gave up and decided the rest of the world will have to change the word to "rickashaw."

Billboards: They have billboards just like us. I see a row of shops as we are traveling on the two-lane blacktop. This area is wood workers who make dressers and headboards. The shops are dirty, makeshift wood and corrugated steel. There is an open sewer running down the road in front of the shops. Overhead is this billboard with a Bangladesh beauty, all decked out in the finest fashions money can buy. She's talking on her cell phone: "Use Bangla-Link for the best ..." the caption declares. What a dichotomy.

Cell phones: I have to talk about cell phones. Everyone has a cell phone. They might not have shoes, and the clothes on their back may be their total net worth, but they have a cell phone. We had visited the islands, which pretty much disappear during the rainy months, and saw how the people lived. Reed huts and reed fences, a few meager belongings that can be transported to higher ground when the floods come. They live a very nomadic and impoverished life. As we were returning to the boat, there was this young man, a teenager, taking our picture with his cell phone. I'm speechless.

Speed bumps: I mentioned there are no traffic lights, none, nowhere, no how. So as a means of controlling the speed of the few vehicles on the roads (as if the congestion wasn't enough, and it wasn't), as you passed through the many villages and towns, they (a road commission of some sort) placed speed bumps across the roads within the towns. So we are barreling along at 35 miles per hour, then slow down to gently roll over the bump, speed up, slow down, another bump, speed up again. Dodge that cart, look out for that ox, bus coming, get back over! A quarter of an inch more and we would not have made it.

Dust: When we travel in Bangladesh, we travel in the dry season. It is dry, very dry. Everything is covered in dust. All the vegetation along our route is covered in brownish grayish dirt. It might be lush in the rainy season if it doesn't get covered by six feet of water.

Smoke and soot: One of the businesses that the people engage in is brick making. The land, being a delta and so wet at times, produces good clay for brick making. The issue is the ovens that are used came out of a different time. They haven't changed the way the bricks are made in many years. Whatever they are burning to heat the kilns to bake the brick causes billowing smoke and soot to paint the landscape with an additional covering of gray. Kind of gets the stuff the dust misses. I have read that the government is moving to make the process greener. That will help the health of the people. It is interesting, watching the workers move the bricks out of the oven. They wear a cap with a flat plate mounted on top, and they pile twelve to fourteen bricks on top of their heads and walk them out. They have got to have strong necks.

Rainy season: In the Chilmary area where we are headed, when it is the rainy season, there is no Chilmary to go to. The rains as well as the melting snows from the Himalayas pretty much keep most of the land under water for six months of the year. The inhabitants of the island area not far from Chilmary pull up stakes and head to higher ground to wait for the waters to recede. They don't have permanent homes, just shacks made of stick and reeds that wash away in the floods. They come back when the water is gone and rebuild and plant their rice, and so it goes round and round. The islands have a tendency to move as well. It's just how the water drains. The joke is, do you want to buy an island? It may not be there when you come back.

Trucks: As we traveled along, we came across these trucks. They looked like a common dump truck that we see in the States. They seemed to be used to carry just about anything: bricks, hay, wood, rice, people, and anything you could picture. Nothing out of the ordinary, however, they were painted and decorated in reds, greens, yellows, blues, oranges, and every bright color you could imagine. The repeated pictures along the side gave you an indication of the function of the truck. Bricks for a brick carrier, rice for a rice carrier, vegetables for a vegetable carrier, and so on. They also didn't move very fast, so we were passing them frequently. As we passed one of the newer ones, my wife exclaimed, "Oh, that is beautiful." My friend and I looked at each other and expressed the same thought: "Beautiful" wasn't the word we had in mind; gaudy, loud, garish, but not beautiful. It's something about the "eye of the beholder," I guess.

Busses: There is public transportation of sorts along the road we're traveling. There are these busses that look like they have been in a demolition derby. Seriously, they are so beat up. They have gouges and scrapes along the sides where they must have grazed something in passing (probably other busses). Few of them have windows other than the windshield. They must be a fairly cheap way of traveling, since they are very crowded. The average bus would hold eighty passengers. There has to be 200 people crammed in the vehicle, on top, and hanging off of the back and sides. I wonder how many people have lost limbs and lives that way. Greyhound it is not.

One-way bridge: We have reached the point in our journey to Chilmary where we have to cross a large river, not a major task, except the bridge only allows one-way traffic. They have a system that opens the gate to traffic one way for ten minutes and then the other way for ten minutes. It was built at a time when there wasn't any vehicular traffic. It is constructed of steel girders, and the roadway is wooden planks, very uneven, since the planks are of different sizes and some are very warped. It's like a road with a lot of large potholes. They are building a new bridge off in the distance that is the replacement, concrete and four lanes. My kidneys hope it's done when I come back.

Cooking: Now, cooking at the Chilmary Medical Center compound is a bit of a challenge. Not that we starve; in fact, the joke is that we are the only team that goes on a trip and gains weight. There is a propane stove with two burners. No ovens, that means no baking or roasting. Those are kind of my specialties.

The first trip I didn't have to deal with that much, as the cooking was handled by others. My second trip there, we had an Iron Chef competition between three of us, which produced three very tasty dishes, none of which I can remember except they all had chicken, which is pretty much all that is available in Bangladesh unless you have a good recipe for goat, which we didn't. We all brought our own secret ingredients from home, since the supplies of herbs and spices is limited, except the local varieties (curry), which we didn't use nor did we want to use. There were three of us, one American, one Chinese, and one Filipino, using Bangladesh vegetables and chicken with our own seasonings. That was an interesting experience.

While we were preparing our creations for the Iron Chef cook-off, there were six of us: three chefs and our designated/volunteer "souse chefs," crammed into the six- by eight-foot area. One stove, two burners, three cooks, cooking three different dishes. Did I mention there were only two pots to cook in? It's a good thing it was a friendly competition. We fussed over everything, right down the garnish for our final presentation. I won, I think.

On my third trip, we had five of us who could be classified as frustrated culinary aficionados, chef wannabes if you will. Needless to say, but I'll say it anyway, the competition took on a different format the second time. We took turns cooking. Each one of us cooked on a different day. We had planned this before we even left, so we had packed into the bags that were checked on through all the special ingredients we would need to create our masterpieces. I had planned on making minestrone, but because of the ingredients I had on hand, I made a modified version I called Banglastrone. It turned out pretty good. They ate it all.

Curry: I have to mention that I am not fond of curry at its best; however, I have to say that the curry they use in Bangladesh is really unpleasant. All meals included rice with curry. It's a poor man's food and we were in a poor man's area, and we ate what they gave us. They felt honored that we ate with them, and we ate what was served. I was honored they shared with us, but I still don't like curry.

Forks: They don't use them. They eat with their right hand, not with their left; never mind why, just not good to do so.

Goat: We saw one tied up outside the kitchen. Didn't think it was a pet, although it had a name; its name was "Lunch." The look it had on its face said as much.

Homeward bound: Back to my first trip. After five days and they were good, productive days, it was time to head home. I came there as a stranger and left my Bangali family behind. I told them I'd be back, and I meant it. So we headed south on the same road over the same one-way bridge, another ten-hour trip, or so we thought.

Bam! About two hours into our trip back to Dhaka, we are traveling as before: passing the slower traffic whenever traffic cleared. This usually works, as I mentioned earlier, but not this day. A truck just a little larger than us decided to make the same move, at the same time. God was with us that day. The collision was head on but not completely head on, otherwise there would have been fatalities. There was a steep embankment to our right, so we couldn't avoid the collision without going over the hill. We had many injuries. The front seat passenger had his leg wrapped in the fender, sprained but not broken, and he was covered in broken glass and bruised and obviously shaken (putting it mildly). The driver was banged up but mobile. One nurse ended up with a broken hip; a doctor had a dislocated elbow; his wife was all banged up. My wife had an injured ankle. I saw what was happening just a split second before the truck hit us and dove on the floor, so I escaped injury, other than being black and blue (for those who do not know what that means, I was just sore a bit).

Now there are no ambulances that you can call to take you to the hospital or police reports to fill out, since there are no police. We are on our own in the middle of nowhere. We gather our wounded into the other van, all sixteen of us, with our injured on the floor, and we head to the nearest hospital, about three hours away. The only pain relief we have is a bottle of Motrin that Vicki and I had packed. We drive on.

What a barn: We arrive at the hospital, and I cannot believe what I see. This place looked like an abandoned factory. No windows, no doors, and dirt on the floor. It is the hospital, though. We are treated kindly and quickly. X-rays are taken and slings and supports applied. They have no pharmacy. The driver has to drive a mile or so to get drugs to help the injured nurse. The people were helpful, kind, and caring but limited in what they could do. An ambulance is located, and we are able to continue to Dhaka. That hospital experience changed us.

Nightmare ride: We travel on. Hour after hour, we drove with the same nerve stretching recklessness that we employed on the way up. This was a nightmare. The injured nurse will have to stay in Dhaka for a month to heal so she can fly home. She had suffered a broken hip. The hospital in Dhaka is a new, state-of-the-art facility where she received top notch care and was the recipient of a few miracles as well. Calls to the US embassy and the consulate get the airlines to hold the plane until we arrive. We say our good-byes and head home.

We had some adventures on the way back home.

Rubber sheets: We get back to Singapore in the early hours of the morning. We have reservations at a highly recommended hotel. We only plan to sleep a short time. We request a wheelchair, usually a standard item at most hotels, and are informed there isn't one. Oh, we have people who need a wheelchair to get to the room; you know, leg injuries and such. We end up using a hand dolly used for luggage and cleaning supplies. What kind of hotel is this? We finally get up to the room: no TV and no radio. No sheets on the bed, just a rubber mattress cover. We call room service to get the bed made; no room service. Okay, I get my wife settled. I go downstairs and sit outside. A businessman walks into the hotel with a woman I at first assumed was his secretary; "Gosh, she's pretty," I think. Another one, with what looks to be his daughter. Traveling with Dad, I guess. Another one, and this one is a Westerner with an extremely beautiful Asian secretary; hey, wait a minute, just what kind of hotel is this? No wonder they only had hourly rates. Turns out the busiest red light district was just three blocks away.

$1,000 wheelchairs: My wife is bummed that she can't go shopping; there is a local market, like a flea market, close by, but she can't walk. So I endeavor to get a wheelchair from a local ambulance service. Sure, they can get us some; I order three, since we have three people who could use them. The cost is about $100. They'll bring them by as soon as the ambulance is free. We wait and wait and call and wait. Finally they show up at three in the afternoon. Good, still time to take Vicki shopping. Just put it on my credit card. They need a deposit. Okay, just put that on my card as well. No, no, we need cash. Okay, how much? I have some money on me. 1,000 Singapore dollars; where am I supposed to get that? I scramble for an ATM and then the money exchanger. Listen, we're leaving tonight at midnight; I need my money back! We'll get it to you. (They did.)

You would think that I would have had enough. That's all I need, thank you very much, God. He sent me back two years later. I'm looking at trip four now, by His grace.

I make light of much of my time in Bangladesh, but that is just how I am. I don't take this life too seriously. We go there to serve, and we get served. We go there to show God's love by loving them, and we receive love. I pray that our visits there can save just one soul, at least one; then I know it is all worthwhile.

"And if anyone gives even a cup of cold water to one of these little ones because he is my disciple, I tell you the truth, he will certainly not lose his reward." Matthew 10:42

(I still don't like the curry).

ACKNOWLEDGMENTS

From the time I presented the idea and told Rick that writing this was something I was told to do, Rick never wavered in support. His response was I think you should. The times I got discouraged he was there to support me and kept me going in the process. Without his love and support I would not have tried this. God has blessed me with a good husband.

I would like to thank my daughter Gina Holben. Your support means more to me than you know. Thanks for the time you went through this work and corrected grammar and made paragraphs out of my writings. Your time was spent making me a better writer. God has blessed me with a good daughter.

What can I say about a son who kept saying "You know Mom it won't be a best seller" when I was worrying about the outcome of my writings. Thank You for allowing me to tell your story. God has blessed me with a good son.

Alyssa and Brittany, I would like to thank you for listening to me. I know sometimes listening to older people can be boring but you did give me support and at times encouragement. God has blessed me with good grandchildren.

To all of my friends who I have traveled with, all of the people who have been a part of this story. I love you and am grateful to you. I have learned from you. We have shared an incredible journey. You are a part of my life. I have named you through this writing so I feel I have acknowledge you, but you must know God has blessed me because of you being in my life. I would like to acknowledge Eun Jin for reading a copy of this book and giving me input some of which I have used. God has blessed me with a sister. A special thanks to Dr. Sang Lee thank you for believing in me. God has blessed me with a brother.

I will always be grateful to the Korean Methodist Church for allowing me a non-member to go to Bangladesh. The church has always made me feel welcome. The church members have always shown me love.

I don't know where I would be without my friends. I would like to acknowledge to following friends; God has blessed me with good friends.

Sharon Lotoczky - thank you for reading the book and for your love and support, you are and have been a part of my life. You have shared my story and have walked through many things with me. God has blessed me because of you.

Ruth Bota - Thanks for the humor in my life and making me learn to hug. You have been a blessing in my life.

Laura Ostrowski - Your love and presence has been something I needed in my life. Thank you for your support and always being honest with me.

Georgann (Gigi) Kelm - Thank you for loving my children a thing which was not always easy. Thank you for sharing your life with me and being honest with me always.

Deanne Kay - Thanks for your support and for reading a copy of this book. Your love and support is a gift in my life. Thanks for your honesty.

Sharon Adams—we have spent many hours together where you have listened to me in the process of my writing. I thank you for your excitement and encouragement in this process and you wiliness to listen to my thoughts. You have helped me clarify my thoughts many times. I am grateful you are in my life.

Kathy Pratt - My artistic friend, what a joy you bring to my life. I love the way you see the colors and the beauty of life. Thank for helping me see the colors.

Susan Todd - God brought you into my life. You are truly my sister. There are not many people that I trust as much as I trust you. We have grown together and both of us are doing things we never saw. God has great plans for you. Keep going.

Debbie Keyes - Thanks for your excitement when we shared about my journey. Even though we live miles away I know that you are just a phone call away. I thank you for listening at a hard time in my life.

Geri H - Thanks for a listening ear and the times you shared your life and love with me.

To my sisters: God has blessed me with good sisters

Chris Kempa - We have been through a lot together. I thank you for always making thing look good, your faith and your love of family. I told you once that God danced on the day you were born and I meant it. I have great love for you.

Judy Ouellette - I thank you for your positive attitude in the face of many trials. Your life has not been easy but you have a determination that cannot be stopped. Your family is blessed to have you.

Mary Wright - We also have been through a lot together. Your caring means a lot to me. Family is important to you. You have been a good mom and I am proud of your for that. The parade company is lucky to have you and I am blessed to have you in my life.

Karen Kuczewski - You are my sister even though you married my brother. Thank you for remembering my mother. Thank you for loving my brother and always being there for my family especially when our brother die.

Fran LaRue - The baby sister. My heart broke for you when Joey died. Life has not been easy for you but you do fit the name "Friendly Fran". Remember I love you.

I would like to thank my nieces and nephews, all of you add so much to my life. I love being an aunt. I love watching you grow and thank you for listening to me. Thank you for your excitement.

Then I have a few people I would like to thank because of their excitement because of my writing;

Jane Kutchey - See Jane I included your last name. Thank you for making my hair look good. Thanks for the title of the book and also thanks for listening.

Rosemary - My friend from swimming. I don't even know your last name but thank you for always asking about the book and your encouragement.

Thank you to all my Engaged Encounter Friends. You have

been there for me when I lacked faith and had much fear. I credit the Encounter as the reason Rick and I are still married. I am grateful for the love you have shown us.

The people I work with; God has blessed me with good co-workers

Kim Marasco - thanks for the encouragement

Geri Flannery - thanks for keeping me going at work.

Linda Kneebone - thanks for the hours you spend looking for supplies that would be throw out so we could use them on the people we visit for medical care , without you we would not been able to do what we were able to do.

Prudi Manzella - thanks for listening and your support

Joyce Webb- thanks for the prayers and your love

Nancy Herman - Thanks for the bake sale

Thanks Donna Craft and Beth Meeker for letting me talk to you in your office many days.

Thanks to the all my MD friends who asked about our trips and your encouraging words.

I would like to thank Dr. Jasmine Ghuznavi for trying to teach me Bengali. Even when I didn't get the words right you kept trying with me. The people in Bangladesh do appreciate the fact I try to speak their langue.

When I started my journey I did not know the people in Bangladesh but I now consisted many of them as friends. I am so grateful for you accepting me and making me feel welcome in my visits.

Words cannot express how grateful I am to Director, Madame Yoo. Madame Chung. I love all of you and always enjoy being with you. God has blessed me in getting to know you.

MEDICAL DICTIONARY

Arrested- The condition of being stopped. Exp cardiac arrest-Irregular heart action.

Billary Ateresia—Closure or obsolesces of some or all of the major bile ducts

Bowel---Intestine

BPD (Bronchopulmonary Dysplasia)- a chronic lung disease primarily affecting premature infants who have been mechanically ventilated; involves air sac damage, scarring of the lung tissue, and area of atelectasis.

Butterflies- (scalp vein)- A specially designed needle for the administration or intravenous fluids, with a flat flange on each side to facilitate anchoring it after placement in a small vein.

Catheter- A tube passed into the body for evacuating fluids or injecting them into body cavities. It may be made of elastic, elastic web, rubber, glass, metal or plastic.

CBG'S (Capillary Blood Gas) A laboratory test performed on blood taken from a capillary (generally by picking the baby's heel) to determine levels of oxygen, carbon dioxide and acid. An important test for evaluating a baby's respiratory status.

Cellulitis- Common skin infection caused by bacteria.

Choanal Atresia—A congenital occlusion of the passage between the nose and pharynx by a bony or membranous structure

Circle Bed-A bed that goes in a circle

Cleft Lip- A Vertical cleft or clefts in the upper lip. This congenital condition results from faulty fusion of the median nasal process and the lateral maxillary processes, is usually unilateral and on the left side, but may be bilateral.

Colostomies- The opening of a portion of the colon through the abdominal wall to its skin surface.

Congential Heart Disease- A disease that is present at birth. Exp. VSD, Transporation of Greater Vessels

Conjoined Twins- Twins that are united

D and C-dilation and curettage- a surgical procedure that expands the cervical canal of the uterus (dilation) so that the surface lining of the uterine wall can be scaped (curettage)

Endotracheal tube (ET tube)- A catheter inserted into the trachea to provide or protect an airway.

Epidermolysis Bullosa- a genetically transmitted form of epidermolysis marked by the formation of deep seated bullae appearing after irritation of rubbing

Foley (Catheter)----A urinary tract catheter with a balloon attachment at an end. After the catheter is inserted, the balloon is inflated. Thus the catheter is prevented from leaving the bladder until the balloon is emptied

Gavage- Feeding with a tube in the stomach or with a tube passed through the nares, pharynx and esophagus into the stomach.

Goiter- An enlarged thyroid gland may be caused by thyroiditis, benign thyroid nodules, malignancy, iodine deficiency, or any condition that causes hyperfunction or hypofunction of the gland.

Hemangioma-Massive raised tumor with blood vessels.

Hernia-The protrusion of an anatomical structure through the wall that normally contains it.

Hymenectomy—In surgery and gynecology, the incision of removal of the hymen

Isolette- A trade name for an incubator. Often used as a common term for and incubator. Incubator-a transparent, boxlike enclosure in which sick or preterm babies are placed. Allows control of temperature around the baby and provides limited protection of the baby from infectious agents.

Imperforated Anus- Condition in which the anus is closed

Nasal Cannula- tubing used to deliver oxygen at levels from 1 to 6 liters/per min. the nasal prongs of the cannula extend approx 1 cm into each naris and are connected to a common tube, which is then connected to the oxygen source.

NEC (necrotizing enterocolitis)- Necrotic- Relating to, or Descriptive of death of a portion of tissue. In this case the portion would be the bowels.

Ostengenesis Imperfect—An inherited disorder of the connective tissue marked by defective bone matrix, short stature and abnormal bone fragility. Additional clinical findings are multiple fractures with minimal trauma, blue sclera, early deafness, opalescent teeth, a tendency to capillary bleeding, translucent skin and joint instability.

Omphalocele (Gastrisis) Congenital hernia of the umbilicus

Prolapse—A falling or Dropping down of an organ or internal part, such as the uterus or rectum.

Pierre Robin—syndrome –unusual smallness of the jaw combined with cleft palate, downward displacement of the tongue and an absent gag reflex

Prune Belly- defect------- A nonstandard but descriptive term for children with congenital absence of one or more layers of abdominal muscles

Pulse oximentry- the use of an oximeter to determine the oxygen saturation of the blood

Respiratory therapy technician—A technician who routinely treats patients requiring noncritical respiratory care and responds to specified respiratory emergencies.

Sitz Bath—The immersion of thighs, buttocks and abdomen below the umbilicus in water

Spinal Bifa (Cystica) –A congenital defect in the walls of the spinal cord caused by lack of union between the laminae of the vertebrae. The lumbar portion is the section chiefly affected.

TAH- Total Abdominal Hysterectomy—Surgical removal of uterus thru the abdomen

Thyroidectomy—Excision of the thyroid gland

Tracheostomy—the surgical opening of the trachea to provide and secure an open airway.

Trisomy--- In genetics, having three homologous chromosomes per cell instead of two

> 13- a serve developmental disorder in which a third copy of chromosome 13 is present in cell nucleus
>
> 18- a serve usually lethal developmental disorder in which a third copy of chromosome 18 is present in the cell nucleus
>
> 21- Down syndrome

Uterus- A reproductive organ for containing and nourishing the embryo and fetus from the time the fertilized egg is implanted to the time the fetus is born.

Medical terms are from the Taber's Medical dictionary used by permission of the F.A. Davis Company.

CPSIA information can be obtained at www.ICGtesting.com
Printed in the USA
BVOW041434310313

316862BV00002B/5/P